CHALLENGING
PUZZLES
IN LOGIC

CHALLENGING PUZZLES IN LOGIC

ROGER HUFFORD

DOVER PUBLICATIONS, INC.
New York

Published in Canada by General Publishing Company, Ltd., 30 Lesmill Road, Don Mills, Toronto, Ontario.
Published in the United Kingdom by Constable and Company, Ltd.

Challenging Puzzles in Logic is a new work, first published by Dover Publications, Inc., in 1982.

International Standard Book Number: 0-486-24224-2
Library of Congress Catalog Card Number 81-68486

Manufactured in the United States of America
Dover Publications, Inc.
180 Varick Street
New York, N.Y. 10014

Contents

Introduction

This is a book about problem solving. Learning to be a good problem solver is like learning to be a good dancer. You don't do it just by watching somebody else, or by reading about the theory. You learn how by trying it yourself. So . . . before we go any further, look at the nine dots in the shape of a diamond in Figure 1. The *problem* is a simple one: start on one of the nine dots, and draw four consecutive straight lines (without lifting your pencil) in such a way that all the dots are connected to at least one other dot with one of your straight lines. The middle diagram shows one person's attempt that failed. Use the other two to try it yourself. If you don't get it on those two diagrams, get another sheet of paper and make your own diamond diagrams.

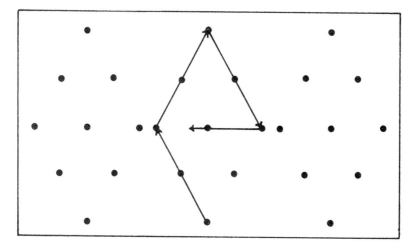

Figure 1.   Connecting nine dots.

If you were successful, congratulations. If you were not successful, then a hint might be in order. When a problem is solvable, and you are not finding the solution, you may be unconsciously restricting your efforts. You are not trying *all* the possible solutions. Try to think of some possible approaches you overlooked in your previous trials. For this particular puzzle, it is quite common for people to assume without thinking that all four straight lines stay inside the borders of the diamond. If you made that assumption, you wouldn't be able to find a solution. Now go back and try again, letting some of your straight lines extend outside the diamond.

If you are still unsuccessful, try drawing four *unconnected* lines (that are not parallel) to connect or at least intersect all the dots. Then see if you can extend the lines in such a way that all four can be connected. Through one method or another, you should be able to find the solution for yourself.

The object of this first problem is to get you to remove the restrictions in your mind against trying new approaches. One of the primary values of problem-solving exercises is to give the solver practice in generating new ways of looking at situations.

Consider a second simple example, one that will require you to use an entirely different method for discovering the solution. In this problem Alf, Bert, and Charlie decide to see if any one of them is psychic. So they take the four aces out of an ordinary deck of cards, shuffle them thoroughly, and place three of them face down on a table. Each person writes down his guess as to the identity of the three cards (see Figure 2). If I tell you that somebody got the right answer each time, that nobody got the right answer every time, and that no two persons ended up with the same number of right answers, you should be able to devise a method for determining what the three aces are that is logical rather than psychic. Try to solve the problem before you read any further.

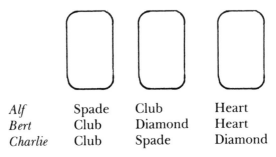

	Spade	Club	Heart
Alf	Spade	Club	Heart
Bert	Club	Diamond	Heart
Charlie	Club	Spade	Diamond

Figure 2.   Who is the psychic?

If you were successful, congratulations. If you were not successful, then, once again, hints might help you. Some problems in this book can be solved by eliminating possibilities. If you can first visualize and chart all the possibilities, then eliminate some of them, you may be able to narrow the field to a single right answer. It looks at first as though there is no good starting place to work out the solution. The clues do tell you, however, that no two persons ended up with the same number of right answers. There are none, one, two, or three possible right answers. One clue says that nobody got the right answer every time, so you can eliminate the possibility of three right answers. Therefore Alf, Bert, and Charlie got, in some order, none, one, and two right answers. Somebody, then, missed all three, and there are only three possibilities for which person it was. Consider the three possibilities one at a time, and determine whether each possibility can satisfy the given conditions or not. Again, try it yourself before you read any further.

Suppose that Alf is the unlucky person who missed on all three guesses. We would then know that the first card would have to be the ace of clubs, and the third card would have to be the ace of diamonds. Then the middle card could not be the ace of clubs or diamonds, and because we know that somebody got the right answer every time, it would have to be the ace of spades. Following that logic, Charlie would have guessed all three correctly (club, spade, diamond). We were told, though, that nobody got all three right, so we now know that Alf could not be the person who missed every time.

Suppose next that Charlie missed all three times. Then the first card is the ace of spades, and the third card is the ace of hearts. The second card is *not* the ace of spades, and must be the ace of diamonds or the ace of clubs. But if it is the ace of clubs, then Alf would have all three right—so that can't be it. Furthermore, if it is the ace of diamonds, then both Alf and Bert would have exactly two right answers, which contradicts the given conditions. We are forced to conclude that it could not have been Charlie who got all three wrong.

It must be Bert who got all three wrong. If Bert missed every time, then the first card must be the ace of spades, and the third card must be the ace of diamonds. Therefore the middle card can't be the ace of spades or the ace of diamonds: it must be the ace of clubs. By this analysis, Alf got two right answers, Charlie got one, and Bert missed every time. This possibility meets the conditions of the problem, and the other two do not, so this must be the right answer.

These two simple introductory problems should demonstrate two very important ideas. The first is the idea of examining all possibilities, rather than unconsciously shutting some of them out of your mind. The person who has the greatest difficulty with real or contrived problems is the person who stubbornly continues to pursue a method that is inappropriate for the situation. In order to solve problems you have to be prepared to consider *all* the possible alternatives, not just the one that looks best initially. The second important idea is using reverse logic to eliminate wrong answers. If you know the total number of possibilities, and the number is small and manageable, you may be able to proceed by examining them one at a time, eliminating those that are inappropriate, and finding yourself at the end with the one answer that fits the conditions of the problem. A word of warning: with real problems, you seldom have all the possible alternatives. A detective who has nine suspects in a murder case, and establishes alibis for eight, may end up hanging the wrong person if a tenth person was the guilty party. With real problems, it is especially important not to close your mind too soon on possible alternatives.

Another important method is intelligent trial and error. When you have identified a number of alternatives, which one should be tried first? There is no rule that guarantees success. You have to develop your own powers of analysis. Sometimes luck plays a part. In order to give you the opportunity to do some trial and error, look at the cryptogram in Figure 3. Each letter in a cryptogram consistently represents a letter of the alphabet; your problem is to find out which one. Trial and error is involved because there are twenty-six possibilities for each letter in the code. Random trial and error would be a time-consuming process, and not much fun. By concentrating on short words, though, and looking for the vowels (every word has one), you reduce the number of trials from twenty-six to four or five, and you should soon hit on the right one.

The problems presented in this chapter should have introduced you to some of the basic tools for problem solving. Whether your problem is a puzzle you are doing for your own amusement, or a

N FONSY ETUPNSZ W ZTTG RLQQUX MWS OXUR CTL

FT W JXFFXA LSGXAEFWSGNSZ TH FOX RATMXEE.

Figure 3. A cryptogram.

political crisis that affects the survival of mankind, some of the
same steps are necessarily involved: getting an understanding of
the elements of the problem, finding the alternative ways the
problem might be handled, testing those alternatives and discard-
ing the unsatisfactory ones, and, finally, knowing when you have
an answer that fits (in a puzzle), or is worth a try (in real life).
Practice in developing the needed abilities on amusing puzzles
should help you prepare yourself to do a better job on real
problems. In that spirit, we offer you for your practice the
following challenging puzzles in logic.

PROBLEMS

Twelve Words a-Hiding

Each problem in this section is a hidden five-letter word. The solver is given a list of guesses as to what the word might be. The number of letters in the guess that appear in the word to be guessed is recorded. For example, if the hidden word is *crust*, and the word *plate* is guessed, the answer would be 1, for the letter T. If a letter occurs two or more times in the word guessed, each occurrence is counted if that letter appears in the secret word, whether it is a multiple in that word or not. For example, if the secret word is *joker*, and *radar* is guessed, the answer would be 2, as two R's in *radar* are letters appearing in the secret word.

This game can be played with two persons guessing alternately, each picking his own secret word. The first person to guess the secret word correctly wins. Of course you lose automatically if it turns out that you accidentally gave an incorrect response to any guess.

WORD ONE		WORD TWO	
Guess	*Answer*	*Guess*	*Answer*
wrong	0	blows	0
value	2	grand	1
hymns	0	wider	1
toxic	1	glaze	0
black	1	pitch	2
topic	2	hardy	1
buffs	0	jokes	1
vivid	1	vivid	0
jilts	1	usual	2
		paper	1

3

WORD THREE

Guess	Answer
zones	1
hymns	0
vague	2
prawn	0
vigor	1
jaded	1
quaff	2
extra	2
going	1
black	0

WORD FOUR

Guess	Answer
pucks	1
grown	2
black	0
fluff	0
vivid	2
paper	1
ozone	0
touch	1
windy	2

WORD FIVE

Guess	Answer
brick	0
night	2
hoped	1
jumps	1
vivid	0
glaze	2
grown	1
mummy	0
score	0
foggy	0

WORD SIX

Guess	Answer
fight	1
quart	1
dizzy	1
vexed	0
rower	0
jewel	0
black	0
moons	0
Japan	1

WORD SEVEN

Guess	Answer
jacks	1
storm	0
vixen	2
laugh	1
blend	2
widow	3
brunt	0
picks	0
ghost	0
vivid	1

WORD EIGHT

Guess	Answer
rivet	1
jerks	1
light	1
beeps	1
facts	1
mound	1
waxed	1
spurs	1
evict	0
might	0

WORD NINE

Guess	Answer
vexed	1
mopes	1
raper	0
moons	1
state	3
queen	0
block	0
proxy	1
fight	3
fuzzy	0

WORD TEN

Guess	Answer
rough	1
testy	2
clamp	1
flops	0
waken	1
hymns	0
jocks	2
godly	0
uvula	0
oxbow	0

WORD ELEVEN	
Guess	*Answer*
flags	1
sport	1
amaze	1
brunt	1
extra	0
jelly	2
chick	0
diver	0
slows	1
zippy	2

WORD TWELVE	
Guess	*Answer*
major	1
queen	1
cover	1
bulky	1
fight	0
drone	1
vital	1
roped	0
lobby	0
zesty	0

Eleven Psychic Guesses

Each problem in this section concerns people trying to guess the identity of cards placed face down on a table. For simplicity, only the aces are used from each suit, with a joker included occasionally. Given the special conditions in each problem, your job is to discover the identity of each card.

FIRST PSYCHIC GUESS

Jack, Queenie, and King deal three aces face down. The guesses of the three are recorded below. Each of the three aces was correctly identified by at least one person. Nobody got just one right answer, however, and no two persons finished with the same number of correct answers.

	First Card	*Second Card*	*Third Card*
Jack	Heart	Spade	Club
Queenie	Heart	Diamond	Club
King	Diamond	Spade	Heart

What Are the Three Cards?

SECOND PSYCHIC GUESS

Encouraged by their previous success, Jack, Queenie, and King try again. This time everybody gets at least one right answer, but no two persons get the same number right.

	First Card	*Second Card*	*Third Card*
Jack	Heart	Spade	Diamond
Queenie	Club	Diamond	Heart
King	Club	Spade	Heart

What Are the Three Cards?

THIRD PSYCHIC GUESS

Ann, Ben, Frank, and Hank agree to test their psychic powers. They use all four aces. Each ace is correctly identified by at least one person. When they check their results, they learn that each of them had the same number of correct guesses.

	First Card	*Second Card*	*Third Card*	*Fourth Card*
Ann	Club	Heart	Spade	Diamond
Ben	Heart	Heart	Diamond	Diamond
Frank	Diamond	Heart	Diamond	Club
Hank	Spade	Diamond	Club	Heart

What Are the Four Cards?

FOURTH PSYCHIC GUESS

Larry, Mary, Perry, and Terry take the psychic determination test. They use the four aces, and each ace is correctly identified by at least one person. When they check their results, they learn that each of them had the same number of correct guesses.

	First Card	*Second Card*	*Third Card*	*Fourth Card*
Larry	Heart	Club	Diamond	Spade
Mary	Club	Spade	Diamond	Heart
Perry	Club	Diamond	Diamond	Club
Terry	Heart	Heart	Club	Spade

What Are the Four Cards?

FIFTH PSYCHIC GUESS

Dolly, Molly, and Polly take the psychic powers test. They shuffle four aces and a joker together. Each card is correctly identified by at least one person. Although nobody ever got two in a row correct, they all ended with the same number of right answers.

	First Card	Second Card	Third Card	Fourth Card	Fifth Card
Dolly	Joker	Heart	Club	Spade	Diamond
Molly	Club	Joker	Diamond	Heart	Club
Polly	Spade	Diamond	Spade	Heart	Joker

What Are the Five Cards?

SIXTH PSYCHIC GUESS

Art, Bart, and Curt enter a competition for psychic guessing with a $50 first prize. They use four aces and a joker. Each card is correctly identified by at least one of the three guessers. Nobody got all the answers right, and nobody got them all wrong. Furthermore, no two of them had the same number of right answers.

	First Card	Second Card	Third Card	Fourth Card	Fifth Card
Art	Spade	Heart	Diamond	Joker	Spade
Bart	Spade	Club	Heart	Club	Diamond
Curt	Diamond	Joker	Spade	Heart	Diamond

Who Won the $50?

SEVENTH PSYCHIC GUESS

Anna, Bella, Carla, and Donna try the psychic determination test, using the four aces and a joker. Each card is correctly identified by at least one person. Nobody got them all right, though, and nobody got them all wrong. At the end, no two persons had the same number right.

	First Card	*Second Card*	*Third Card*	*Fourth Card*	*Fifth Card*
Anna	Club	Joker	Heart	Diamond	Club
Bella	Diamond	Joker	Heart	Club	Spade
Carla	Heart	Club	Spade	Diamond	Joker
Donna	Diamond	Joker	Club	Club	Spade

What Are the Five Cards?

EIGHTH PSYCHIC GUESS

Alex, Bob, and Chris persuade Don to try their psychic powers test with them. Each card is correctly identified by at least one person. Nobody got them all right, and nobody got just two right. No two of them ended up with the same score.

	First Card	*Second Card*	*Third Card*	*Fourth Card*	*Fifth Card*
Alex	Joker	Diamond	Heart	Spade	Club
Bob	Club	Spade	Heart	Joker	Diamond
Chris	Club	Diamond	Joker	Spade	Club
Don	Heart	Joker	Heart	Club	Spade

What Are the Five Cards?

NINTH PSYCHIC GUESS

Brandy, Candy, Randy, Sandy, and Uriah test their psychic powers, using four aces and a joker. Each of the five cards was guessed correctly by one or more of the persons guessing. At the conclusion, four persons were tied in the number of correct guesses. The one person not tied with the others had one less correct answer.

	First Card	Second Card	Third Card	Fourth Card	Fifth Card
Brandy	Club	Joker	Diamond	Club	Heart
Candy	Joker	Spade	Club	Spade	Joker
Randy	Club	Club	Heart	Diamond	Joker
Sandy	Heart	Diamond	Diamond	Joker	Club
Uriah	Spade	Heart	Joker	Spade	Diamond

What Are the Five Cards?

TENTH PSYCHIC GUESS

Allen, Ben, Curt, Dirt, Ed, and Fred take the psychic determination test. They use just four aces. Although nobody got all the answers right, there was a clear winner. Two men were tied for second and third, and two others were tied for fourth and fifth. Nobody got none right.

	First Card	Second Card	Third Card	Fourth Card
Allen	Spade	Spade	Club	Diamond
Ben	Heart	Diamond	Diamond	Club
Curt	Diamond	Club	Heart	Spade
Dirt	Diamond	Heart	Spade	Club
Ed	Heart	Spade	Club	Diamond
Fred	Club	Spade	Diamond	Heart

What Are the Four Cards?

ELEVENTH PSYCHIC GUESS

Alice, Brenda, Carol, Diane, and Elaine take the psychic determination test. They use four aces and a joker. At least one person got the right answer for each of the five cards. When they checked their answers, all five had the same number of right answers.

	First Card	Second Card	Third Card	Fourth Card	Fifth Card
Alice	Spade	Heart	Club	Joker	Diamond
Brenda	Spade	Joker	Diamond	Club	Spade
Carol	Club	Diamond	Spade	Joker	Heart
Diane	Diamond	Heart	Joker	Club	Spade
Elaine	Club	Joker	Diamond	Spade	Heart

What Are the Five Cards?

Ten Digits Coded

Each of these problems represents a problem in simple arithmetic, with letters substituted for the ten digits. Of course the code is different for each problem, but in each problem the same letter always represents the same digit. Your job is to find out which letter stands for which digit in each problem. You can check your solution by first confirming that you have always substituted the same number for a letter wherever it appears, and then doing the arithmetic problem to ensure that it works out.

FIRST CODE

```
    H  E  A  R  T
 +  S  P  A  D  E
    ─────────────
    T  R  U  M  P
```

SECOND CODE

```
    W  H  E  A  T
 +     G  E  R  M
    ─────────────
    G  R  A  I  N
```

THIRD CODE

```
       S  N  O  W
 +     W  I  N  D
    ─────────────
    S  T  O  R  M
```

FOURTH CODE

```
       R  O  C  K
 +  M  U  S  I  C
    ─────────────
    C  H  A  R  M
```

FIFTH CODE

```
       E  I  G  H  T
 +     S  E  V  E  N
    ────────────────
    T  W  E  N  T  Y
```

SIXTH CODE

```
    M  A  I  N  E
 +     I  O  W  A
    ─────────────
    T  E  X  A  S
```

13

SEVENTH CODE

```
    M A I N E
+   I D A H O
  ─────────────
  O R E G O N
```

EIGHTH CODE

```
      T E X A S
+     I D A H O
    ─────────────
    K A N S A S
```

Why is no answer possible?

NINTH CODE

In the following division problem, when the digits are arranged in order from 0 to 9, they spell a word or phrase.

```
                    A G O
D I A L  /T H R E A D
          G A L O
          ───────────
          A L I E A
          A L D G L
          ───────────
          A I G D
```

TENTH CODE

In this division problem, it is clear that Moe is a normal male. When the digits are arranged in order, however, you should be able to tell what his favorite sport is.

```
                  M O E
M A L E  /N O R M A L
          U L R N
          ───────────
          E D N A
          M A L E
          ───────────
          O H D U L
            A N O D
```

Nine Baseball Problems

It is not necessary to be a baseball fan to solve the problems in this section. The problems do not involve substitutes or pinch hitters or bench strength, but concern only the starting nine players on a particular day. Three outfielders play right field, center field, and left field. The infielders play first base, second base, shortstop, and third base. The pitcher throws the ball, and the catcher catches it. That's all the special baseball knowledge you will need. The rest of the challenge depends on your ability to think in a logical and orderly fashion.

THE TUCSON TERRIERS

Art, Bart, Chet, and Dan are the infielders for the Tucson Terriers. Their batting averages for the season, in no particular order, are .350, .300, .250, and .200. All the players are truthful when they speak about who plays which position, but when they speak about batting averages, those who hit below .300 always lie. Those who hit .300 or better, naturally, always tell the truth.

Art   Dan is hitting .250.
          Chet's average is higher than Bart's.

Bart   Dan is not the shortstop.
          Art's batting average is higher than the second baseman's.

Chet   The first baseman is hitting .350.
          The .250 hitter is not the third baseman.

Dan   My batting average is .250.

Determine Each Player's Position and Batting Average.

THE $6 MILLION INFIELD

Jack, Ken, Larry, and Mel are the infielders for the world's champion Bluesox. During their most successful season, each of them led the league in one of the following: home runs, RBI's, batting average, or stolen bases.

1. Mel had a higher batting average than the stolen-base champion.
2. Ken and the third baseman often had dinner with the RBI leader.
3. Jack and the shortstop were friends of the home run leader.
4. Larry did not lead the league in RBI's.
5. Jack did not play second base.
6. Larry and the home run leader were roommates, and generally had the room next to the second baseman and the third baseman.
7. The third baseman did not lead the league in stolen bases.

Determine Which Position Each Man Played, and What He Led the League in.

THE BROOKLYN BASHERS

The Brooklyn Bashers were incredible hitters, averaging better than ten runs a game. Nevertheless, their pitching and catching were so weak that they lost every game. Not surprisingly, when they socialized with strangers at a bar after a game, the pitcher and catcher lied when they talked about which players played which positions. Everyone else told the truth.

Ron	Yuri is shortstop.
Seth	Ximenes is the catcher.
Tad	Zeb is the center fielder.
Uriah	Tad is the first baseman.
Van	Seth is the pitcher.
Warren	Uriah is the right fielder.
Ximenes	Van is the third baseman.
Yuri	Ron is the left fielder.
Zeb	Warren is the second baseman.

Who Played Each Position?

THE LOUISVILLE LUMBERJACKS

The Louisville Lumberjacks were wonderful hitters and fielders, but lost every game due to the weakness of their pitching and catching. Therefore, when the nine starters talked to friends about the game afterward, it is not surprising that the pitcher and catcher lied when they talked about who played which position. All the other players told the truth.

Jake	Nick plays third base.
Ken	Owen is the pitcher.
Len	Sam is the right fielder.
Mack	Paco is the shortstop.
Nick	Rick plays second base.
Owen	Ken is the left fielder.
Paco	Len is the catcher.
Rick	Jake plays first base.
Sam	Mack is the center fielder.

Who Played Each Position?

THE PHOENIX PHIZZLES

The Phoenix Phizzles had tremendous hitting and fielding, but lost every game due to bad pitching and catching. When they dined after a game, the nine starters often discussed with strangers about who had done what during the game. It is not surprising that the pitcher and catcher lied when they talked about who played which position, but the other seven told the truth. Brad is *not* the left fielder, and Iggie is *not* the shortstop.

Brad	Elvis is the shortstop.
Chet	Hank is the center fielder.
Dave	Judd plays third base.
Elvis	Gregg is the pitcher.
Finn	Chet plays first base.
Gregg	Iggie is the left fielder.
Hank	Finn plays second base.
Iggie	Brad is the catcher.
Judd	Dave is the right fielder.

Who Played Each Position?

THE INDIANAPOLIS INVERTS

The Indianapolis Inverts have brought up a whole new infield from their Peoria farm club. All the infielders, the pitcher, and the catcher lie whenever they talk about which players play which positions. Only the outfielders tell the truth.

Zeke	Will is the pitcher. Ule is not the third baseman.
Yaz	Vic is the shortstop. Tom is not the first baseman.
Xerxes	Sam is the catcher. Vic is not the pitcher.
Will	Rick is the center fielder. Xerxes is not the left fielder.
Vic	Tom is the right fielder. Yaz is not the second baseman.
Ule	Zeke is the third baseman. Sam is not the catcher.
Tom	Yaz is the left fielder. Rick is not the right fielder.
Sam	Xerxes is the second baseman. Zeke is not the center fielder.
Rick	Ule is the shortstop. Will is not the left fielder.

What Position Does Each Man Play?

THE VICKSBURG VERACITIES

The Vicksburg Veracities were a very popular team because they were more truthful than most. All of them can be trusted to tell the truth when they say what position a man *does not* play. All of them, except for the three outfielders, who always lie when making positive statements, tell the truth when they say what position a man *does* play.

Abner	Hank plays right field. Ernie is not the center fielder.
Ben	Ernie plays first base. Dick is not the first baseman.
Chris	Frank is the right fielder. Abner is not the second baseman.
Dick	Abner is the pitcher. Frank is not the third baseman.
Ernie	Chris plays center field. Ben is not the shortstop.
Frank	Chris plays shortstop. Ian is not the centerfielder.
Gus	Dick is the catcher. Chris is not the catcher.
Hank	Chris is the left fielder. Gus is not the catcher.
Ian	Gus plays second base. Hank is not the pitcher.

What Position Does Each Man Play?

THE PERFIDIOUS POTTSTOWN PELICANS' PITCHER AND CATCHER

The Pottstown Pelicans' infielders always tell the truth and their outfielders always lie. The trouble comes with the pitcher and the catcher, who alternate between lying and telling the truth from one statement to the next. You can't even be sure whether their first statement will be a true one or a false one.

Matt	Yuri is the right fielder. Will is the catcher.
Nat	Pat is the shortstop. Will is the right fielder.
Pat	Matt is the catcher. Stan is the first baseman.

Ron	Yuri is the pitcher. Tim is the third baseman.
Stan	Pat is the pitcher. Tim is the shortstop.
Tim	Matt is the second baseman. Ron is the center fielder.
Will	Zeke is the third baseman. Stan is the center fielder.
Yuri	Nat is the first baseman. Zeke is the left fielder.
Zeke	Nat is not an infielder. Ron doesn't pitch or catch.

Who Is the Left Fielder?

THE INCONSISTENT IBERIA ICON INFIELDERS

The Iberia Icon outfielders always lie, and their pitcher and catcher always tell the truth. Their infielders, however, are not even considerate enough to lie all the time, but instead make statements that are alternately true and false (every other statement being false). One cannot even assume that the first statement an infielder will make will be true; it is possible for his first statement to be false and his second true.

Frank	Rick is the center fielder. Ike is the pitcher. Jack is the right fielder.
Hank	Mike is the center fielder. Nick is the third baseman.
Ike	Frank is the catcher. Hank is the second baseman.
Jack	Kirk is the third baseman. The pitcher is not always truthful.

Kirk	Nick is the catcher.
	Mike is the shortstop.
	Hank is the right fielder.
Luke	Rick is the shortstop.
	The infielders always lie.
Mike	Kirk is the first baseman.
	The shortstop never lies.
Nick	Luke is the left fielder.
	Ike is the second baseman.
Rick	Jack is the left fielder.
	Luke is the pitcher.
	Frank is the first baseman.

What Position Does Each Man Play?

Eight Leagues of Hockey

You do not need to be a hockey fan to solve the hockey problems in this section. For each puzzle, some of the information is missing or incorrect. Your job is to find what is missing in order to learn the scores of all the matches.

Two points are awarded to the winning team in a hockey match. In case of a tie, both teams are awarded one point, so the total points in the standings should always equal the total number of games played (since each game played is counted as one for each of the two participating teams). Of course, total goals scored for and total goals scored against must be the same, since every goal scored for one team is scored against another.

THE NOVICE HOCKEY ASSOCIATION

The Novice Hockey Association is for beginners. Just three teams are in the league, and each plays the other two teams just once. Only part of the information appears in the results chart.

Team	Games	Won	Lost	Tied	Goals For	Goals Against
A	2			1	0	
B	2	1			1	2
C	2					

Determine the Score of Every Match.

THE WOMEN'S HOCKEY ASSOCIATION

The Women's Hockey Association consists of just four teams. The first season each team played every other team once. At the end of the season the Belles were in first place with five points, the Colleens had three points, and the Angels had one point. A total of nine goals was scored in all the matches; the Dames scored

22

none. The Belles were high in goals scored with four. The Colleens allowed a total of only three goals for all three matches, and defeated the Angels three to two.

What Was the Score When the Belles Played the Angels?

THE JUNGLE HOCKEY LEAGUE

Recent excavations have established that a hockey league once flourished in an ancient civilization now overrun by jungle. Some of the records have been obliterated by jungle rot, but historical research has established that there are only two mistakes in what remains. The information given below shows the standings part way through a season in which every team was ultimately to play every other team just once. D has already played B, A has played E, B did not have two ties, and the highest scoring match was the one between B and E.

Team	Games	Won	Lost	Tied	Goals For	Goals Against	Points
A	3				0	1	1
B	3				3	1	4
C	3				1		3
D	3			2	1		3
E	3			0			2

Determine the Score of Every Match Played Thus Far.

DUST BOWL HOCKEY

I got interested in Dust Bowl hockey when I watched the Sidewinders win a match two to one. So I got hold of the two newspapers that cover the Dust Bowl and discovered that each paper kept accurate records of its own three teams in the league, but had every figure wrong about the teams covered accurately by the other paper. The league was set up so that each of the six teams was to play each of the five rivals just once.

Teams	Games	Won	Lost	Tied	Goals For	Goals Against
SAND SENTINEL						
Asps	5	4	0	1	5	0
Boas	5	3	1	1	6	2
Cobras	5	3	2	0	5	9
Pythons	3	2	1	0	4	1
Rattlers	5	1	1	3	1	1
Sidewinders	4	0	4	0	0	8
DAILY DUST						
Asps	4	2	2	0	6	1
Boas	4	2	2	0	2	3
Cobras	4	0	3	1	1	4
Pythons	4	3	0	1	3	6
Rattlers	4	3	0	1	8	2
Sidewinders	5	1	3	1	2	6

Determine the Score of Every Match.

A MONSTROUS HOCKEY PROBLEM

Monsters, just like everybody else, love to play hockey, and the roughness of the sport does not deter them. Their two newspapers, however, are terribly inaccurate: each paper reports three of the teams correctly in every detail and gets the other three completely wrong; so it is necessary to consult both to determine the actual scores. This is important to me, because the monsters have offered me a free ticket for next week, and I want to choose the big game. Each team meets every other team just once during the season. Assume that the Alligators will win their game with the Lizards next week, but also lose a game before the season ends.

Team	Games	Won	Lost	Tied	Goals For	Goals Against
			GHOUL'S GAZETTE			
Alligators	3	1	2	0	3	2
Bats	4	0	4	0	0	6
Crocodiles	4	0	2	2	1	4
Dragons	5	4	1	0	5	2
Goats	4	1	0	3	4	2
Lizards	3	3	0	0	4	1
			POTION PRESS			
Alligators	2	0	1	1	2	3
Bats	5	2	2	1	2	4
Crocodiles	5	3	1	1	6	1
Dragons	4	1	2	1	2	5
Goats	5	2	3	0	1	4
Lizards	5	2	1	2	6	2

Determine the Score of Every Match Played Thus Far, and Tell What Match Will Decide the Championship.

SLOBBOVIAN HOCKEY

Most Slobbovians love hockey, and I am no exception. I have a ticket for the final game of the season next week, between the Elks and the Fangs. Each of the three major metropolitan areas in Slobbovia has two hockey teams, and the six teams in the league each play the other teams once during the season. Unfortunately, the press is not very reliable. The paper in each city keeps accurate records on how their own two teams are doing, but their reports on the other four teams in the league are totally wrong on every figure reported. The standings as carried in the three papers are listed below.

Team	Games	Won	Lost	Tied	Goals For	Goals Against

DILLON DAILY SNOWBALL

Team	Games	Won	Lost	Tied	Goals For	Goals Against
Apes	5	2	0	3	3	1
Bulls	3	3	0	0	7	1
Condors	5	2	2	1	3	6
Dogs	5	2	2	1	4	1
Elks	4	1	2	1	3	3
Fangs	4	0	4	0	0	8

FROZEN FREE PRESS

Team	Games	Won	Lost	Tied	Goals For	Goals Against
Apes	4	1	2	1	1	2
Bulls	4	1	1	2	4	4
Condors	3	3	1	0	7	2
Dogs	4	1	3	0	2	5
Elks	3	2	1	0	2	5
Fangs	5	3	2	0	4	2

GHASTLY GAZETTE

Team	Games	Won	Lost	Tied	Goals For	Goals Against
Apes	3	0	1	2	4	4
Bulls	5	2	2	1	5	3
Condors	4	1	0	3	2	1
Dogs	3	3	0	2	3	1
Elks	5	0	3	2	1	4
Fangs	3	1	1	1	1	4

Determine the Scores of All Games Played This Season.

ALL THE NEWS THAT'S FIT TO PRINT

In our local hockey league all the teams are scheduled to play each other just once. Before the final week of the season I decided to take the day off to watch the game between the Chiefs and the Eagles. I asked our cub reporter to prepare the standings for the paper. I phoned in the results of the match I watched—a scoreless tie. I've seen just one Chiefs match this year that wasn't a tie. When the paper appeared the next day a fan called in to tell me that every figure given was wrong. When I asked the cub about it, he protested that he had checked the figures to be sure they were right. I asked him how he did the checking, and he told me he had added the columns to be sure the totals were correct. Sure enough, every column total was what it should have been, but all the information on the table was wrong just the same. Teams earn two points for each win, and one for a tie. Here are the standings as they appeared in the paper:

Team	Games	Won	Lost	Tied	Points
Apes	4	0	2	2	3
Braves	4	2	0	2	4
Chiefs	3	1	1	1	4
Devils	2	1	0	1	0
Eagles	3	0	1	2	5

What Are the Correct Standings? What Matches Are to Be Held Next Week?

ALL GREEK

The ancient Greeks were noted for their fierce partisanship, but it is nonetheless remarkable that their chronicles were not always correct about the hockey standings. In fact, each of the two papers carried correct information only about the two teams that were its favorites, and every item was wrong regarding the other three teams in the league. This meant that for one of the teams *neither* paper had correct information on any of the items. The schedule consisted of each team playing every other team in the league once. The following information appeared before the season was completed:

Team	Games	Won	Lost	Tied	Goals For	Goals Against
PELOPONNESIAN PRESS						
Argo	3	2	0	1	2	0
Boeotia	3	0	3	0	2	4
Corinth	2	2	0	0	3	1
Delphi	4	2	1	1	1	2
Epirus	4	1	3	0	2	3
SPARTAN SENTINEL						
Argo	4	0	2	2	1	2
Boeotia	4	2	0	2	3	0
Corinth	3	0	1	2	2	2
Delphi	3	1	2	0	2	4
Epirus	3	2	0	1	4	4

Determine the Correct Standings.

If I give you the further information that one of the teams, against all odds, has had every match this season end with the identical score (though they did not win every match), you should be able to:

Give the Score of Every Match Played This Season.

Seven Days of Racing

Each problem in this section requires the solver to determine which horses won in various races. Use the information given to cross out horses that have lost and to circle those that have won. It will probably be easiest to work right on the book itself, but you can copy the bets on another piece of paper if you prefer.

MONDAY

Five secretaries—Pat, Queenie, Rhoda, Sal, and Tess—go to the racetrack, but only in time for the last five races. Their bets are indicated on the chart below. Every secretary picked a winner, but no two picked the same number. Two of them are overheard making statements afterward, both of which are true:

Tess   Queenie picked twice as many winners as I did.

Queenie   And I know I also won more than one other secretary.

Race

	First	Second	Third	Fourth	Fifth
Pat	Aardvark	Beowulf	Cedric	Derek	Falange
Queenie	Ariana	Belinda	Cedric	Derek	Fizz
Rhoda	Aardvark	Belinda	Cedric	Doorknob	Freedom
Sal	Ariana	Beowulf	Cedric	Derek	Fizz
Tess	Aardvark	Beowulf	Chester	Doorknob	Fizz

Name the Five Winning Horses and the Most Successful Secretary.

29

TUESDAY

Five secretaries went to the racetrack and bet on five races. At least one secretary picked the winner for every race. The one who did the worst won only one race fewer than the others (except the one who did best), and the one who did best won only one race more than the others (except the one who did worst). There was only one race in which most of the women picked the winner. No one won both the second and fifth races, or both the first and third races.

Race

	First	Second	Third	Fourth	Fifth
Donna	Picardy	Ribald	Samurai	Tornado	Vandal
Eva	Pocono	Ronin	Saki	Toggle	Vesper
Freda	Peony	Ribald	Samurai	Tornado	Vandal
Greta	Picardy	Ribald	Shogun	Tempest	Vandal
Hedda	Pocono	Rancho	Shogun	Tornado	Vesper

What Five Horses Won? Which Secretary Picked the Most Winners?

WEDNESDAY

The women could not get off work early enough to see all the races, but they did make it in time to bet on the last six. They did well, with at least one of them picking the winner in each race. Nobody won two races in a row, however, and no two women won together more than once. At the end of the day, everyone had picked the same number of winners. Wompus did not win the sixth race.

Race

	Third	*Fourth*	*Fifth*	*Sixth*	*Seventh*	*Eighth*
Ada	Tidal	Uranus	Vibrate	Warlord	Yellow	Zebulon
Bess	Trump	Upset	Vasco	Whisper	Yonder	Zig-Zag
Cassie	Tidal	Uranus	Vasco	Warlord	Yolande	Zither
Dora	Trump	Uvula	Victor	Warlord	Yellow	Zither
Ella	Tidal	Uvula	Victor	Wompus	Yolande	Zig-Zag
Flossie	Twist	Uranus	Vasco	Whisper	Yellow	Zither

Name the Six Winners.

THURSDAY

Though at least one of seven secretaries picked the winner in each race on Thursday, no one was able to win two races in a row. Gloria never won when Ida did, and Hattie never won when Jean did. At the end of the day, one of the women had won only in odd-numbered races, and one had won only in even-numbered races. All but one of the women tied with the same number of wins, and that one lucky secretary won two races more than anyone else. The lucky winner was one of the women who won only in odd- or even-numbered races.

Race

	First	Second	Third	Fourth	Fifth	Sixth	Seventh	Eighth
Gloria	Alien	Bon-Bon	Coyote	Dibs	Erewhon	Fuller B	Gem	Haircut
Hattie	Alpha	Bourbon	Coolie	Desire	Evasion	Firefly	Gandy	Hideout
Ida	Alpha	Bourbon	Coyote	Dogma	Ersatz	Fuller B	Gem	Happy
Jean	Alien	Bourbon	Caper	Dogma	Evasion	Foamy	Gilda	Hideout
Karla	Aurora	Broom	Coyote	Dibs	Ersatz	Firefly	Gem	Haircut
Laura	Alpha	Bon-Bon	Cygnus	Dibs	Erewhon	Foamy	Gilda	Hideout
Mona	Alien	Blondie	Coolie	Dibs	Evasion	Foamy	Gilda	Happy

What Eight Horses Won? Which Secretary Picked the Most Winners?

FRIDAY

On Friday at least one secretary picked the winner in each of the races, though in only two races did most of them win. More than once two or more of the women picked the winner in the same race, but no two won together more than once (that is, if Sarah and Trixie both picked the winner in the first race, then afterward whenever Sarah picked a winner Trixie did not, and whenever Trixie picked a winner Sarah did not). Surprisingly, at the end of the day all the women had the same number of winners. Even stranger, though, was the fact that one of them won only odd-numbered races, while another won only even-numbered ones.

Race

	First	Second	Third	Fourth	Fifth	Sixth	Seventh	Eighth
Sarah	Garland	Handy	Ironize	Jackal	Kinky	Lola	Miracle	Narrows
Trixie	Gamin	Handy	Ideal	Jocko	Kulak	Laser	Miracle	Nuisance
Una	Gorilla	Hayburn	Ignition	Jazz	Kinky	Linkage	Miser	Nick-Nack
Violet	Gamin	Handy	Ironize	Jutland	Kargon	Linkage	Miser	Narrows
Wanda	Gorilla	Hayburn	Ideal	Jutland	Kinky	Lola	Miracle	Nuisance

Name the Eight Winning Horses.

SATURDAY

Saturday at least one secretary picked the winner in each of the races. One woman at the end of the day had one winner more than all the rest (who were tied). It was noted that Cathy never won when Ellie did, and Dotty never won when Francie did, nor did Annie ever win when Dotty did. Annie won just once when Betty did, and Cathy won only once when Francie did. Strangely enough, one woman won only in the odd-numbered races, and another won only in the even-numbered races. Only once did three or more secretaries who bet on the same horse win. Edgy did not win the fifth race.

Race

	First	*Second*	*Third*	*Fourth*	*Fifth*	*Sixth*	*Seventh*	*Eighth*
Annie	Advance	Bella	Careful	Dum-Dum	Elfin	Folly	Goodbar	Hopeful
Betty	Aces	Bella	Careful	Deft	Elfin	Fairway	Gala	Hopeful
Cathy	Alice	Barge	Caution	Dum-Dum	Easier	Finian	Goodbar	Hopeful
Dotty	Aces	Bait	Corky	Doily	Elfin	Finian	Gesture	Headless
Ellie	Advance	Bella	Careful	Deft	Edgy	Finian	Goodbar	Hopeful
Francie	Aces	Barge	Corky	Deft	Easier	Folly	Gesture	Harlan

Name the Eight Winners and the Most Successful Secretary.

SUNDAY

All the secretaries went to the racetrack on their day off and bet $5 on each of the first five races. They also put $5 apiece in a pot, to go to the person who picked the most winners in the five races. After the fifth race, however, all five had picked the same number of winners. The secretaries voted to give half the money to the only one who had lost money on the first five races, and to return $2.50 to each person who had put $5 in the pot. Thus only one secretary came out behind for the day (counting the bets on the five races and the money each woman put in and took out of the pot).

Race

	First	*Second*	*Third*	*Fourth*	*Fifth*
Joan	Whirlybird 2–1	Argon 2–1	Bolero 2–1	Crouton 5–1	Drudgery 3–1
Kaye	Wagoneer 3–1	Amnesty 3–1	Blastoff 3–1	Cabal 3–1	Dirty Dingo 3–1
Laura	Whirlybird 2–1	Avalanche 4–1	Bolero 2–1	Cabal 3–1	Dark Prince 2–1
Marge	Wellby 5–1	Argon 2–1	Bedelia 5–1	Cinnamon 4–1	Drudgery 3–1
Nell	Wagoneer 3–1	Amnesty 3–1	Bolero 2–1	Cabal 3–1	Dirty Dingo 3–1

Which Horses Won? Which Two Secretaries Made the Most Money? How Much?

Six Leagues of Prophets

The next six problems concern the National League East many years in the future. Each year, before the season begins, the six teams all make predictions about how the season will end. Those who predict accurately do not necessarily finish first in the standings, but neither do they always finish last, so the owners are probably mistaken in their belief that ballplayers are too concerned about prophets.

It will be your job to determine from the information given how the teams finished in the final standings each year.

1993

The 1993 season provided excellent evidence that it is not wrong for baseball players to be concerned about prophets. Each team of the National League East predicted how two other teams would finish. The only team that was correct with both predictions finished first. The only other team to make a correct prediction was the team that finished second.

Cardinals	The Cubs will finish second. The Pirates will be fifth.
Cubs	The Pirates will take first. The Expos will be second.
Expos	The Mets will be first. The Phillies will be sixth.
Mets	The Cardinals will be first. The Expos will be fourth.
Phillies	The Cubs will finish fifth. The Mets will be third.
Pirates	The Phillies will be third. The Cardinals will finish fourth.

Determine the Position of Each Team in the Final Standings.

1994

In 1994 each team of the National League East made predictions about how two other teams would finish. At the end of the season the team in first place was the team with two correct predictions. and the teams in second and third each had one correct prediction. The teams finishing fourth, fifth, and sixth were wrong on both of their predictions, so it was clear in this instance at least that good prophets made for winning baseball. The Mets finished ahead of the Pirates.

Cardinals   The Cubs will be sixth.
                      The Expos will be fifth.

Cubs   The Phillies will be third.
                      The Mets will be fifth.

Expos   The Pirates will be first.
                      The Cardinals will be sixth.

Mets   The Expos will be third.
                      The Phillies will be fourth.

Phillies   The Pirates will be fourth.
                      The Mets will be second.

Pirates   The Cardinals will be first.
                      The Cubs will be second.

Determine the Position of Each Team in the Final Standings.

1995

In 1995 each team of the National League East predicted how two other teams would finish. At the end of the season, it turned out that both predictions made by the team that finished first were true, one of the two predictions made by the team that finished second was true, and all other predictions were false. The Cubs did not finish ahead of the Expos, the Expos were not second, and the Phillies did not finish last or second.

Cardinals   The Expos will be third.
                      The Pirates will be fourth.

Cubs	The Expos will be fifth.
	The Mets will be sixth.
Expos	The Cards will be fifth.
	The Cubs will be fourth.
Mets	The Cards will be fourth.
	The Phillies will be third.
Phillies	The Pirates will be third.
	The Cards will be sixth.
Pirates	The Mets will be third.
	The Cubs will be fifth.

Determine the Position of Each Team in the Final Standings.

1996

In 1996 each team of the National League East predicted how the other teams would finish. Of the twelve predictions, five turned out to be correct. Just one team was wrong on both predictions, and that team finished last.

Cardinals	The Phillies will be second.
	The Cubs will be sixth.
Cubs	The Cardinals will be fourth.
	The Pirates will be first.
Expos	The Mets will be second.
	The Cardinals will be sixth.
Mets	The Cubs will be fifth.
	The Phillies will be fourth.
Phillies	The Pirates will be third.
	The Expos will be first.
Pirates	The Mets will be third.
	The Expos will be fifth.

Determine the Position of Each Team in the Final Standings.

1997

In 1997 each team of the National League East predicted how the other teams would finish. Only the team that finished last was correct on both of its predictions. The team that finished fifth had one correct and one incorrect prediction. All the other teams were wrong about both predictions. The Phillies did not finish fifth.

> *Cardinals*   The Pirates will be sixth.
> The Expos will be first.
>
> *Cubs*   The Cardinals will be fourth.
> The Pirates will be third.
>
> *Expos*   The Mets will be sixth.
> The Phillies will be second.
>
> *Mets*   The Cardinals will be first.
> The Cubs will be fourth.
>
> *Phillies*   The Mets will be second.
> The Cubs will be fifth.
>
> *Pirates*   The Expos will be fifth.
> The Phillies will be third.

Determine the Position of Each Team in the Final Standings.

1998

In 1998 each team of the National League East predicted how the other teams would finish. Only the team that finished last was correct on both of its predictions. The team that finished fifth had one correct and one incorrect prediction. All the other teams were wrong about both predictions. The Pirates did not finish fourth.

> *Cardinals*   The Phillies will be sixth.
> The Cubs will be fourth.
>
> *Cubs*   The Expos will be fifth.
> The Mets will be second.

Expos	The Cardinals will be first.
	The Phillies will be third.
Mets	The Cardinals will be fourth.
	The Pirates will be first.
Phillies	The Expos will be second.
	The Pirates will be third.
Pirates	The Cubs will be fifth.
	The Mets will be sixth.

Determine the Position of Each Team in the Final Standings.

Five Poker Hands

Given twenty-five playing cards dealt at random, what are the odds that you will be able to arrange them into five hands of five cards each so that all five will be "pat" hands? Given the "deals" of twenty-five cards in this section, and assuming a "pat" hand is one a player would not discard from in hopes of improving it (a straight or better), your task will be to arrange the cards into five pat hands.

FIRST POKER PROBLEM

Spades	2, 3, 6, 7, 8, 9, 10, Q, K, A
Hearts	5, 10, Q, K, A
Diamonds	2, 3, 6, 7, 9, J
Clubs	3, 4, 10, A

SECOND POKER PROBLEM

Spades	2, 3, 6, 7, 9, Q, K
Hearts	2, 3, 4, 5, 6, 7, 9, Q, K
Diamonds	2, 3, 4, 5, 6
Clubs	2, 3, 4, K

THIRD POKER PROBLEM

Spades	4, 5, 7, 8, 9, J, K, A
Hearts	2, 3, 4, 6, 7, 8, 10, J
Diamonds	6, 7, 9, K, A
Clubs	4, 6, 7, 8

FOURTH POKER PROBLEM

Spades	2, 3, 6, 10, Q
Hearts	5, 9, Q, K, A
Diamonds	2, 4, 5, 8, 10, J, Q
Clubs	2, 3, 5, 9, 10, J, Q, A

FIFTH POKER PROBLEM

Spades	4, 5, J
Hearts	2, 4, 6, 7, 8, 9, J
Diamonds	4, 5, 8, 10, Q, K, A
Clubs	2, 5, 6, 7, 9, J, Q, K

Four Secret Codes (Cryptograms)

One form of cryptogram is a coded message in which each letter is always represented by the same code letter. It is not necessary for you to send in 25¢ and a box top for a Captain Midnight decoder ring to decipher the messages. One-letter words will have to be *a* or *I*, two-letter words will always have a vowel in them (perhaps a *y*), and two-letter words rarely end in *a* or *i* or *u*. Watch for double letters in a word, and frequently used words like *the* and *that*, or words ending in *ing* or *s*. By trial and error and a few shrewd guesses, you should be able to read the messages.

Although cryptograms are a very common type of puzzle, they are included here because they are quite useful in gaining an understanding of the problem-solving process, particularly the role of trial and error. You may learn the most from a cryptogram when you start out with some wrong assumptions. It is a good idea to use a very light pencil so that you can make changes easily if you discover you are on the wrong track.

FIRST CRYPTOGRAM

X N V X H D V W Z G H S P V E X H S W Z G Y

Z Q S K L H J H X H V E Q H J J Y V X G Y S K

T H S V C H P H C V S C.

SECOND CRYPTOGRAM

V C Y V S W T Y T L U E Y O W W T G C A O

W V M Y L U C G O U Y O N Y Z W S V U

W T V O Y R T V E G O L A U Y Y R G W T X V Q.

THIRD CRYPTOGRAM

QCZLRKLUL   CHLU   BKL   UFWPMCR...FP
FLUCQCJ   QIUFS   WQ   ELQBUCSWPN
BKL   CGCPL   JFSLU.

FOURTH CRYPTOGRAM

WFQZUE   KUZQRC   KDUQV: EZGZU
YDGZ   VF   WDEO   FNZQ   VF   WMKY   CF
VF   PZN.

Three History Tests

The three problems in this section are intended to be whimsical rather than historically accurate. Don't bother to look up information in your history textbooks, but just apply your problem-solving techniques to determine the answers. There are no tricks, and statements that seem to agree do agree, and those that seem to contradict do, in fact, contradict. The problems are presented in order of difficulty, not chronologically.

THE FAMOUS FLASH FLOOD

Noah, sensing from the pain in his corns that bad weather was brewing, got one of his sons to help him build a boat, and the whole family went off on a trip. As with most vacationing families, they were constantly nagged by the worry that they had forgotten something. They talked about it all the time, and not always truthfully. No two of them, in fact, made the same number of true statements among the comments listed below. If I tell you that nobody made exactly three true statements, you should be able to resolve an important historical dilemma.

Noah	1. Shem forgot to lock the door.
	2. Ham helped me build the boat.
	3. My wife forgot to snuff the candles.
	4. The boys did not sneak any extra animals aboard.
Mrs. Noah	5. I snuffed all the candles.
	6. We put all the children on the ark.
	7. I turned off the major faucets.
	8. Shem locked the door.
Shem	9. We left my little sister at home.
	10. I locked the door.
	11. My brother and I sneaked extra cows aboard—for steaks.
	12. Ham is the oldest son.

Ham
13. I helped daddy build the boat.
14. Momma forgot to turn off the major faucets.
15. My brother and I sneaked extra cows aboard—for steaks.
16. My brother is older than I am.

Did Mrs. Noah Remember to Turn Off the Major Faucets?

THE NOTORIOUS NYMPH OF THE NILE

Recent archaeological studies have provided a translation of some cryptic hieroglyphic inscriptions. They are statements made by Cleopatra, her father, Marc Antony, and Julius Caesar. Not all the statements are true; in fact, no two persons made the same number of true statements. Assume that all the statements were made the same day, that Cleopatra could truly love only one person at a time, that someone told more lies than Julius Caesar did.

Cleopatra
1. I lost my asp in Memphis.
2. My heart belongs to daddy.
3. I do not love Julius.

Antony
4. Cleo loves me.
5. Caesar is ambitious.
6. Brutus is a true friend of Caesar's.

Julius
7. Cleo loves me.
8. Brutus is a true friend.
9. Cleo did not lose her asp in Memphis.

Cleo's Dad
10. Cleo loves Marc Antony or Julius Caesar.
11. Cleo lost her asp in Memphis.
12. Caesar is not ambitious.

Whom did Cleopatra Love?

THE GARDEN OF EDEN

Everything was perfect in the Garden of Eden, until one day somebody ate an apple from the tree of knowledge. The immediate result was that you could no longer trust people to tell the truth. In fact, when the residents were questioned about the event, only one of them answered all the questions truthfully. All the others told some lies, though no two of them told the same number of lies.

Adam
1. The snake ate the apple.
2. The snake was in the garden.
3. Eve has not weeded the garden.
4. Abel failed to do his chores.

Eve
5. Adam ate the apple.
6. We are not all equally truthful.
7. I was out weeding the garden.
8. The snake lies.

Cain
9. Abel ate the apple.
10. Abel doesn't always tell the truth.
11. Mother has always preferred Abel.
12. The snake never lies.

Abel
13. Cain ate the apple.
14. The snake can't see over the hedge.
15. I have done my chores.
16. The snake ate the apple.

Snake
17. I was not in the garden.
18. Eve ate the apple.
19. Cain is Eve's favorite son.
20. I can't see over the hedge.

Who Ate the Apple?

Two Tournaments

The following two problems come from the world of speech competition. They are fictitious, though, and no special knowledge of speech activities is required. They can be solved with the same problem-solving techniques used for the previous problems.

THE ORATORY CONTEST

Alice, Beth, Cindy, Diane, and Ella agree to compete in an oratory contest, to be judged by Fred, George, Hal, Ian, and Jim. Each judge is to rank the five contestants, giving a 1 to the best speaker, 2 to the second best, and so on through number 5. Then the numbers of the ranks are to be added up, and the speaker with the lowest total will be the winner.

When the ranks were added up, no two speakers were tied.

1. Everybody got one first-place vote.
2. Everybody but Alice got one fifth-place ranking. Ella was ranked fifth twice.
3. Fred ranked Ella above Diane, but below Alice.
4. One judge ranked the five girls 1–5 in alphabetical order.
5. Ian gave Beth last, and Diane first.
6. Beth's total score was 15.
7. Jim gave Ella first.
8. If Ella had received the rank George gave Cindy, and Cindy had received the rank George gave Ella, Ella would have won first place and Cindy would have been last (with no ties).
9. George gave Diane second and Alice third.
10. Fred gave Diane fourth.
11. Beth got a higher rank from Jim than from George.
12. Jim ranked Cindy higher than Alice.

Who Won the Oratory Contest?

THE DEBATE TOURNAMENT

Twelve teams attended a five-round debate tournament at Hardware U. The teams are identified by number in the schedule

48

below. The schedule indicates which teams competed in each of the five rounds, and, where indicated by an asterisk, which rounds were judged by Professor Files, the coach of team 1. The schedule was determined by chance in the first two rounds, but the next three rounds were "power-matched," which means that insofar as possible, teams with identical records were scheduled to meet each other. Power-matching is not always possible; for example, if there are five teams with 2–0 records at the end of two rounds, four of them could meet in two debates, but the fifth would have to meet the top team with a 1–1 record.

The tournament director announced with rounds 3 and 4 that the power-matching was perfect, that is, every team met a team with an identical record. When he put up the schedule for round 5, he announced that only one undefeated team was left in the tournament, and that only four of the six debates were perfect matches. After round 5, the director announced that no undefeated team remained.

The director went back to tabulate results. A fire in the tab room, caused by an improperly extinguished cigarette, burned not only the ballots but also the tournament director. Only the speaker awards escaped the conflagration. Speaker awards are used to break ties if two teams finish with the same win-loss record. Two speakers from team 12 took the top two awards, followed by two from team 9, then two from team 11, and finally two from team 7.

Professor Files voted for team 6 in round 1, team 10 in round 2, team 2 in round 3, team 12 in round 4, and team 11 in round 5. Everyone agreed that the most important thing was to determine which team won the tournament (the deceased director would have wanted it that way). Professor Files examined the pairings, then announced that he knew who won.

Round 1			*Round 2*		
Affirmative	*Negative*	*Judge*	*Affirmative*	*Negative*	*Judge*
1	2		2	3	
3	4		4	5	
5	6	*	6	7	
7	8		8	9	
9	10		10	11	*
11	12		12	1	

Round 3				Round 4		
Affirmative	*Negative*	*Judge*		*Affirmative*	*Negative*	*Judge*
1	10			3	5	
2	9	*		11	2	
4	7			12	8	*
5	12			7	1	
6	11			9	6	
8	3			10	4	

Round 5		
Affirmative	*Negative*	*Judge*
1	9	
2	12	
6	3	
7	10	
8	5	
11	4	*

Which Team Received the First-Place Trophy?

And a Final Matrimonial Mess

Your final problem should present a real challenge, and matrimonial messes can certainly do that. Work with care to solve this one.

CONFUSION CONDOMINIUM

Five couples live in Confusion Condominium. Their lives are made difficult by the fact that one of the five men makes his living as a thief. The other four husbands are a rich man, a poor man, a beggar man, and a doctor. One member of each couple always tells the truth and the other always lies. In four of the five couples, it is the wife who tells the truth and the husband who lies. The only husband who always tells the truth is the poor man, as you might suspect. A further complication is that all ten persons have names that can designate men or women. In the statements made below by the ten persons, nobody mentions the name of his own spouse.

Bobby	1. Pat is married to Terry.
Ellie	2. Kim is married to the rich man.
Freddie	3. Ellie is married to Ronnie.
Jerry	4. Ellie is married to Willie.
	5. Freddie is the beggar man.
Kim	6. Jerry is not married to Terry.
Lou	7. Pat is not the poor man.
	8. Bobby is married to Jerry.
Pat	9. Freddie is married to Ronnie.
	10. Willie is not the doctor.
Ronnie	11. Jerry is either the rich man, or Jerry is a woman.
	12. Bobby is married to Kim.
Terry	13. Freddie is married to Lou.
	14. Ellie is a woman.

51

Willie   15. Kim is the thief.
              16. Freddie tells the truth.

Who Is the Thief?

II

SOLUTIONS

Solutions to Twelve Words a-Hiding

WORD ONE	taped	WORD SEVEN	waxed
WORD TWO	truck	WORD EIGHT	labor
WORD THREE	quiet	WORD NINE	sixth
WORD FOUR	wrist	WORD TEN	trick
WORD FIVE	plant	WORD ELEVEN	plump
WORD SIX	puffy	WORD TWELVE	knack

Solutions to Eleven Psychic Guesses

FIRST PSYCHIC GUESS

1. Since nobody got just one right, and no two persons had the same number of right answers, then one person had three right, one person had two right, and one person had no right answers.
2. If Jack had three right, Queenie would have two right and King one right. This must be rejected, as we know nobody had just one right.
3. If King had three right, Jack had just one right, so this possibility must be rejected.
4. If Queenie had three right, Jack had two right, and King had none right. This meets the given conditions, and must be the correct answer.

Answer:
Heart, Diamond, Club

SECOND PSYCHIC GUESS

1. With everybody having a right answer, and no two having the same number, the number of correct answers must be three, two, and one.
2. If Jack got three right, Queenie would have none. This is impossible.
3. If Queenie got three right, Jack would have none. This is impossible.
4. King must have three right. This gives Queenie two right and Jack one.

Answer:
Club, Spade, Heart

THIRD PSYCHIC GUESS

1. The correct card was picked by at least one person each time. If the card most frequently picked was always correct, there would be eight correct answers. But diamonds were most frequently picked twice, and

could not be correct twice. Therefore the maximum number of correct answers is seven.

2. Since all had the same number of right answers, the total must be divisible by four. We can conclude there must have been exactly four right answers.
3. Therefore no more than one answer is right for any pick.
4. Heart, then, must be false for the second card. Hank is right; it is a diamond.
5. Hank, then, must be wrong about the first, third, and fourth cards. The third card cannot be a diamond; and, since Hank is wrong about the third card, it must be the ace of spades.
6. Since the fourth card cannot be a diamond or Hank's guess, it must be a club.
7. The first card, by elimination, has to be the ace of hearts.

Answer:
Heart, Diamond, Spade, Club

FOURTH PSYCHIC GUESS

1. The total number of right answers must be divisible by four, since everyone had the same number right. There must be more than four right answers, since for the first card there must be two right answers. There must be less than twelve, since twelve would require an average of three right answers, and only once did all three guess the same card. We can conclude each person got two right.
2. Because only one answer was right for the second card, there must be two for the first card, three for the third, and two for the fourth to get the required total of eight right answers.
3. Diamond, then, has to be right for the third card and spade for the fourth. Since Larry got them both, he must be wrong for the first and second cards, and the first card must be a club.
4. By elimination, the second card is the ace of hearts.

Answer:
Club, Heart, Diamond, Spade

FIFTH PSYCHIC GUESS

1. There were at least five correct answers. The total number must be divisible by three, since all three people had the same number correct. Therefore there must be exactly six correct answers, since there are not enough duplicate guesses to make nine possible.
2. In order to have six correct answers, heart must be correct for the fourth card.
3. To avoid two correct in a row, the third card has to be club, and the fifth card has to be diamond.
4. The second card can't be a heart, as that would make two in a row for Dolly, so it must be joker.
5. By elimination, the ace of spades is the first card.

Answer:
Spade, Joker, Club, Heart, Diamond

SIXTH PSYCHIC GUESS

1. Since no two had the same number right, the number of correct guesses must be either four, three, and two; three, two, and one; four, two, and one; or four, three, and one. Therefore a minimum of six guesses must be correct for the five cards, thus we know that at least one card was guessed correctly by two persons—either the first or the fifth card.
2. If spade is correct for the first card, it can't be for the fifth card, so the fifth card must be a diamond. Similarly, if diamond is correct for the fifth card, it can't be for the first card, so the first card must be a spade. Since one of the two alternatives must be correct, for purposes of deduction we can conclude that they both are (and that there will be seven total correct answers).
3. The third card cannot be a diamond or spade, since they have already been located. By elimination, the third card must be a heart.
4. Cards two and four must be the club and the joker. Though we do not know which is which, since Bart guesses club both times, he must be correct on one or the other. Therefore he has a total of four correct guesses and wins the $50.

Answer:
Bart

SEVENTH PSYCHIC GUESS

1. Since nobody got all right and nobody got all wrong, and no two had the same number of right answers, the four girls had, in some order, four, three, two, and one correct guesses, for a total of ten right answers.
2. The second card is either a club or the joker. If it is a club, and the most common guess is correct every other time, there would be only nine correct answers. Therefore the second card must be the joker.
3. The fifth card can't be the joker, so it must be a club or a spade.
   A. If it is a club, then the fourth card must be the diamond, the first card would have to be the heart, and the third card would have to be the spade. This yields just eight right answers, so the fifth card can't be a club.
   B. The fifth card, therefore, is a spade. Thus the third card has to be a heart or a club.
      1. If it is a club, then the fourth card must be a diamond, and the first card must be a heart. This yields only nine right answers, so the third card can't be a club.
      2. The third card is therefore a heart.
4. Either the first card is a diamond and the fourth a club, or vice versa.
   A. If the first card is a diamond and the fourth a club, Bella has all five right. This contradicts the given conditions and must be false.
   B. Therefore the first card is a club and the fourth is a diamond.

Answer:
Club, Joker, Heart, Diamond, Spade

EIGHTH PSYCHIC GUESS

1. The number of correct answers must be four, three, one, and none, in some order.
2. The persons with three and four right must have at least two identical guesses. This can't be Alex and Bob, Alex and Don, Bob and Chris, Bob and Don, or Chris and Don. By elimination, Alex and Chris (in some order) have four and three right answers.
3. Therefore either Bob or Don had none right.
4. If Don had none right:
   A. The third card would have to be the joker.
   B. The fourth card is not the joker or Don's guess. It must be a spade.
   C. The second card, then, can't be joker or spade; it must be a diamond.
   D. The fifth card can't be spade or diamond; it must be a club.
   E. The first card can't be joker or club; it must be a heart. But that gives Don a right answer. We can conclude Don could not be the one who got them all wrong. It must be Bob.
5. If Bob had none right:
   A. The third card must be the joker.
   B. The second card is not the joker or Bob's guess; it must be a diamond.
   C. To have eight right, there must be two correct answers for cards one and four, or one and five, or four and five.
      1. It can't be done for cards one and five, as club is picked twice both times.
      2. It must be for cards one and four or four and five. Either way, the fourth card is a spade.
   D. The fifth card, by elimination, is a club, and the first card must be a heart.

Answer: Heart, Diamond, Joker, Spade, Club

NINTH PSYCHIC GUESS

1. If four of the five persons were tied at the first card, the fifth person would have no right answers, and it would not be possible for someone to be correct on each of the five cards (which would require a minimum of five right answers).
2. If four of the five were tied at the third card (the fifth person having two right answers), there would have to be fourteen right answers. If the card most often picked each time is right, the maximum number of right answers is nine. We can conclude that four of the five must be tied with two right answers, with the fifth person having one right answer, and that the card most often guessed must be correct each time.
3. Therefore the first card must be a club, the third must be a diamond, the fourth must be a spade, and the fifth the joker. By elimination, the second card must be a heart.

Answer: Club, Heart, Diamond, Spade, Joker

TENTH PSYCHIC GUESS

1. Since nobody got them all right, the "clear winner" must have had three right, two men had two right, two men had one right, and one man missed them all—a total of nine correct guesses.
2. The most frequently guessed card is guessed only twice for the first card, three times for the second card, twice for the third card, and twice for the fourth card. In order to have nine correct guesses, the most frequently guessed card must be the right answer each time. This tells us the second card must be a spade, and in trials one, three, and four, the right answer is a card guessed by two persons.
3. Since the second card is a spade, spade can be crossed out for trials three and four. Heart can also be crossed out, since only one person guessed heart. Therefore the third card must be either a diamond or a club, and similarly the fourth card must be a diamond or a club. By elimination, then, the first card *can't* be a diamond or a club and must be a heart.
4. Either the third card is a club and the fourth a diamond, or the other way around. If the third is a club and the fourth a diamond, Ed would have four right answers. Therefore the third card must be a diamond and the fourth a club.

Answer: Heart, Spade, Diamond, Club

ELEVENTH PSYCHIC GUESS

1. There are one or two possible correct answers for each card, or a maximum of ten right answers.
2. All five girls had a maximum, then, of two right answers apiece, a situation that obtains only if the "favorite" card was the correct answer each time.
3. If the favorite card is ever incorrect, however, each girl must have only one right answer, and the single choices would have to be correct each time. If so, the answers to the five trials are, in order, diamond, diamond, unknown, spade, and diamond. Since it is impossible for the ace of diamonds to be three places at once, each girl must have two right answers, and all the single answers are wrong.
4. Therefore the correct answer for the third card must be diamond. Diamond, then, is wrong everywhere else.
5. Carol is wrong, we know now, about the second and third cards, but must be right about two of the three others.
   A. Carol can't be right about both the fourth and fifth cards, as that would mean all the guesses about the second card would have to be wrong.
   B. Carol can't be right on trials one and four, as this would mean three correct answers for Elaine.
   C. Therefore, by elimination, Carol is right about the first and fourth cards.
6. By elimination, the heart is the second card; the spade is the fifth.

Answer: Club, Heart, Diamond, Joker, Spade

Solutions to Ten Digits Coded

(Other answers may be possible on addition problems.)

FIRST CODE

```
    6 8 1 5 9
   (H E A R T)
 + 2 7 1 4 8
  (S P A D E)
   9 5 3 0 7
  (T R U M P)
```

SECOND CODE

```
    3 6 5 0 9
   (W H E A T)
 +   4 5 1 8
    (G E R M)
   4 1 0 2 7
  (G R A I N)
```

THIRD CODE

```
    1   5 8 9
   (S   N O W)
 + 9   2 4 7
   (W   I N D)
 1 0   8 3 6
  (S T O R M)
```

FOURTH CODE

```
    8 3 6 9
   (R O C K)
 + 5 2 4 1 6
   (M U S I C)
   6 0 7 8 5
  (C H A R M)
```

FIFTH CODE

```
    8 0 5 2 1
   (E I G H T)
 + 6 8 3 8 9
   (S E V E N)
 1 4 8 9 1 0
  (T W E N T Y)
```

SIXTH CODE

```
    6 9 4 8 3
   (M A I N E)
 +   4 1 0 9
    (I O W A)
   7 3 5 9 2
  (T E X A S)
```

SEVENTH CODE

```
    9 3 8 5 4
   (M A I N E)
 + 8 0 3 6 1
   (I D A H O)
 1 7 4 2 1 5
  (O R E G O N)
```

EIGHTH CODE

There are more than ten letters.

NINTH CODE

```
0 1 2 3 4 5 6 7 8 9
O R A D E L I G H T
```

TENTH CODE

```
0 1 2 3 4 5 6 7 8 9
H O M E R U N L A D
```

Moe's favorite sport is baseball.

Solutions to Nine Baseball Problems

THE TUCSON TERRIERS

1. Dan says his average is .250, but if it were, he would lie about it. Therefore he lies, and must be the .200 hitter.
2. Art says Dan is batting .250, which is a lie. Art, then, lies about averages. Since he is not the .200 hitter, he must be the .250 hitter.
3. Since Dan and Art lie about their averages, Bart and Chet must be the .300 and .350 hitters. Art, who lies about batting averages, says Chet's average is higher than Bart's. Since this is a lie, Bart's average must be higher, so Bart is hitting .350 and Chet is hitting .300.
4. Chet says the first baseman is hitting .350, so Bart must play first base.

5. Bart says Art's batting average is higher than the second baseman's. We know only Dan is hitting less than Art, so Dan must play second base.
6. By elimination, Art must play shortstop or third base. Chet says the .250 hitter (Art) is *not* the third baseman, so he must be the shortstop.
7. Chet, then, by elimination, must play third.

Answer:	*Player*	*Position*	*Average*
	Art	Shortstop	.250
	Bart	First base	.350
	Chet	Third base	.300
	Dan	Second base	.200

$6 MILLION INFIELD

1. Set up a diagram indicating which men cannot play certain positions, which cannot win certain titles, and which positions do not go with titles.

	First Base	*Second Base*	*Short-stop*	*Third Base*	*Home Runs*	*RBI's*	*Stolen Bases*	*Average*
Jack		No	No		No			
Ken				No		No		
Larry		No		No	No	No		
Mel							No	
Home Runs		No	No	No				
RBI's				No				
Stolen Bases				No				
Average								

2. Where three negative answers appear, the fourth possibility must be correct, so we know the first baseman was home run champion and the third baseman had the highest average.
3. Since Larry and the home run leader lived next to the second and third basemen, they must have played first base and shortstop. If the first baseman is home run leader, Larry must be the shortstop.
4. Since the third baseman was batting champion, Larry (the shortstop) must have led the league in stolen bases.
5. Since Jack did not win the home run championship, he could not have been first baseman, therefore he must have played third and been batting champion.
6. By elimination, Mel had to lead the league in RBI's.
7. Ken is left with first base and the home run championship. Mel must be the second baseman.

Answer:

Player	Position	Achievement
Jack	Third base	Highest batting average
Ken	First base	Home run leader
Larry	Shortstop	Stolen base leader
Mel	Second base	RBI leader

THE BROOKLYN BASHERS

1. If Van tells the truth:
   A. Seth is the pitcher, and therefore lies.
   B. Ximenes, then, is *not* the catcher (or pitcher), so he must tell the truth.
   C. Van, therefore, is the third baseman.
   D. One person, and only one, other than Seth, lies.
      1. Tad, Zeb, Warren, and Uriah each make statements about the next man: Tad identifies Zeb, Zeb identifies Warren, Warren identifies Uriah, and Uriah identifies Tad. If any of the four were the catcher, he would lie, but the person who identifies him would also have lied. Therefore all four must have told the truth.
      2. Similarly, Ron and Yuri identify each other. If either lies, that man would have to be catcher, and the other would have lied as well. We know therefore that both must have told the truth.
   E. If Van tells the truth, we know the following:

C		2B	Warren	LF	Ron
P	Seth	SS	Yuri	CF	Zeb
1B	Tad	3B	Van	RF	Uriah

   F. By elimination, Ximenes must be the catcher. This shows that our original assumption that Van tells the truth must be false.
2. Van is therefore the pitcher or the catcher.
3. Ximenes, then, lies about Van, and must also be the pitcher or catcher.
4. Seth, then, must tell the truth. We know Ximenes is catcher, so Van must be pitcher.
5. All the others tell the truth.

Answer:

C	**Ximenes**	**2B**	**Warren**	**LF**	**Ron**
P	**Van**	**SS**	**Yuri**	**CF**	**Zeb**
1B	**Tad**	**3B**	**Seth**	**RF**	**Uriah**

THE LOUISVILLE LUMBERJACKS

1. Ken says Owen is the pitcher. If Ken lies, he must be the pitcher or catcher, and Owen must also be telling a lie, which would mean that Owen would have to be the catcher and Ken the pitcher. But Paco says Len is the catcher, which would make three lies, and there can be only

two. Therefore Ken must be telling the truth, and Owen is the pitcher.
2. Similarly, Paco says Len is the catcher. If Paco lies, Mack must also lie, and that is impossible, since it would make three lies (with Owen's lie). Therefore Paco tells the truth, and Len must be the catcher.
3. Filling in the seven known positions leaves only left field and right field undetermined, and only Ken and Sam unplaced. Since Owen lies when he says Ken is the left fielder, Ken must be the right fielder. Similarly, when Len says Sam is the right fielder, we know by elimination he must be the left fielder.

Answer:

P	Owen	2B	Rick	LF	Sam
C	Len	SS	Paco	CF	Mack
1B	Jake	3B	Nick	RF	Ken

THE PHOENIX PHIZZLES

1. Chet identifies Hank, Hank identifies Finn, and Finn identifies Chet. If anyone lies, he is the pitcher or catcher, and the one identifying him also lies. Since two others identify persons as pitcher or catcher, this would, make four lies. Therefore Chet, Hank, and Finn all tell the truth.
2. Similarly, Dave and Judd identify each other: both must be telling the truth.
3. The two lies have to be in the four statements made by Brad, Elvis, Gregg, and Iggie. There are six possible ways the statements could have been made:

		1	2	3	4	5	6
Brad:	Elvis is shortstop	F	F	F	T	T	T
Elvis:	Gregg is pitcher	F	T	T	F	F	T
Gregg:	Iggie is left fielder	T	F	T	F	T	F
Iggie:	Brad is catcher	T	T	F	T	F	F

A. The third column is impossible, as it has Gregg, identified truly as pitcher, telling the truth.
B. The fourth is impossible, as it has Brad, truly the catcher, telling the truth.
C. The fifth is impossible, as it has Iggie, the left fielder, telling a lie.
D. The sixth has Gregg pitcher. Iggie lies about Brad and must be catcher. Brad and Elvis tell the truth, so Elvis is shortstop and Brad is left fielder. But we were given that Brad is *not* left fielder, so the sixth possibility cannot be correct.
E. The second possibility is Gregg is pitcher and Brad the catcher. Iggie is not in left field, so he would be shortstop. Elvis is in left field. We were given that Iggie is *not* the shortstop, so the second column cannot be correct.
F. By elimination, the first column is correct. Iggie is left fielder, Brad is catcher. Elvis lies about Gregg; therefore Elvis must be the pitcher. Gregg must be the shortstop.

Answer:

P	Elvis	2B	Finn	LF	Iggie
C	Brad	SS	Gregg	CF	Hank
1B	Chet	3B	Judd	RF	Dave

THE INDIANAPOLIS INVERTS

1. Tom either tells the truth or lies. Either way he identifies one of the outfielders.
   A. Assume Tom tells the truth:
      1. Yaz is the left fielder.
      2. Yaz tells the truth, so Vic is the shortstop.
      3. Vic lies, then, about Yaz, and Yaz must be second baseman.
      4. Yaz could not be both the second baseman and the left fielder; therefore we know that Tom did not tell the truth.
   B. Therefore we know that Tom lies, and
      1. Rick must be the right fielder.
      2. Rick tells the truth, so Ule is shortstop.
      3. Ule lies, so Sam is catcher.
      4. Sam lies, so Zeke is center field.
      5. Zeke tells the truth, so Will is pitcher.
      6. Will lies, so Xerxes is left field.
      7. Xerxes tells the truth: Sam is catcher; but this is not new information.
      8. We have identified three outfielders, so Vic, Yaz, and Tom all lie.
         a. Vic lies, so Yaz must be second base.
         b. Yaz lies, so Tom is first base.
         c. By elimination, Vic is third base.

Answer:

P	Will	2B	Yaz	LF	Xerxes
C	Sam	SS	Ule	CF	Zeke
1B	Tom	3B	Vic	RF	Rick

THE VICKSBURG VERACITIES

1. Three outfielders lie about what position a man plays, therefore there is a total of three lies in statements saying what position a man does play.
2. Ernie says Chris plays center field, Frank says Chris is shortstop, and Hank says he is left fielder. Clearly two of the three lie and, thus, are outfielders.
3. Abner says Hank plays right field, Chris says Frank is the right fielder; so Abner or Chris must be the third outfielder. It follows that the other four are *not* outfielders. Ben, Dick, Gus, and Ian must have told the truth. Ernie, then, is first base, Gus is second base, Abner is the pitcher, and Dick is the catcher.
4. Now we know Ernie must have told the truth, so Chris plays center

field. Frank and Hank, who lied about Chris, must be the other outfielders.
5. Ben and Ian are left with shortstop and third base, and because Ernie says Ben is not the shortstop, Ben must be third base and Ian shortstop.
6. Chris lies when he says Frank is the right fielder, therefore Frank must be the left fielder.
7. Hank has to be the right fielder: Abner (the pitcher) told the truth.

Answer:

P	Abner	2B	Gus	LF	Frank
C	Dick	SS	Ian	CF	Chris
1B	Ernie	3B	Ben	RF	Hank

THE PERFIDIOUS POTTSTOWN PELICANS'
PITCHER AND CATCHER

1. With each player making two statements, there must be ten true statements and eight false ones (four infielders each make two true, the pitcher and catcher each make one true).
2. There is a total of eight pairs of contradictory statements (such as "Tim is the shortstop" and "Tim is the third baseman."). Since one of each pair must be false, yielding the maximum possible of eight false statements, the two statements about Ron, which do not contradict, must both be true, and Ron is the center fielder.
3. Ron lies about Yuri and Tim, so Matt tells the truth about Yuri; thus Yuri is the right fielder. Stan tells the truth about Tim: he is the shortstop.
4. Tim, then, tells the truth, and Matt is the second baseman.
5. Matt, then, tells the truth, and Will is the catcher.
6. Yuri lies about Nat and Zeke (first base and left field), and Will must tell the truth when he says Zeke is the third baseman.
7. Since Will is the catcher, every other of his statements is a lie. He must lie about Stan being the center fielder.
8. We know Nat's statement about Pat is false, and his statement about Will is false. Therefore Nat must be an outfielder, and since right field and center field have already been established, Nat must be the left fielder.
9. To complete the analysis, Pat lies about Matt and tells the truth about Stan. Thus Pat is the pitcher and Stan the first baseman.

Answer:
Nat is the left fielder.

THE INCONSISTENT IBERIA ICON INFIELDERS

1. Every player makes at least two statements, so there are at least eight true statements (the pitcher and catcher make two each, infielders one each), and at least ten false statements.
2. Of the twenty-one statements, there are nine pairs of contradictories, and three statements that are clearly false (the second statements by Jack, Luke, and Mike) because they contradict given conditions. At a

minimum, eight of the nine contradictory pairs must contain true statements.

3. Therefore either one of the two statements about who is pitcher, or one of the two statements about who is catcher, *must* be correct (there may be one correct in each pair).
   A. Assume Kirk tells the truth when he says Nick is the catcher.
      1. Then Nick tells the truth: Luke is the left fielder and Ike plays second base.
      2. If Ike plays second, he makes one false and one true statement. The false one would have to be that Hank plays second, so it would have to be true that Frank is the catcher. This contradicts our beginning assumption that Nick was catcher. Clearly Nick *cannot* be catcher.
   B. Assume Ike tells the truth when he says Frank is catcher.
      1. Then Frank tells the truth: Ike is pitcher, Rick plays center field, and Jack plays right field.
      2. Since Frank makes three statements (all true), there will be a total of nine true statements. One of each contradictory pair will have to be true.
4. If Ike is pitcher, his true statements confirm that Frank is catcher, and also tell us that Hank plays second.
5. Luke lies when he says that Rick is the shortstop (we know now he plays center field), and his second statement is also a lie. Luke must be an outfielder, and since center and right have already been determined, Luke must play left.
6. Hank lies when he says Mike plays center, therefore he must tell the truth when he says Nick plays third.
7. Kirk lies about Nick and Hank, so his second statement must be true: Mike is the shortstop.
8. Mike's second statement is a lie, so his first must be true: Kirk plays first.

Answer:

P	Ike	2B	Hank	LF	Luke
C	Frank	SS	Mike	CF	Rick
1B	Kirk	3B	Nick	RF	Jack

Solutions to Eight Leagues of Hockey

THE NOVICE HOCKEY ASSOCIATION

1. B scores only one goal, yet wins a game. Must have won 1–0. B therefore gave up two goals in their other game and lost 0–2.
2. A plays a tie (it must have been with C, as we know B had a win and a loss). Since A scores no goals, the tie must have been 0–0.
3. When A plays B, again they score no goals, so A must have lost 0–1.
4. C's game with B, then, must have been a 2–0 victory for C.

Answer: *Contestants*
                          _____

Game	A	B	C
1	0	1	. . .
2	0	. . .	0
3	. . .	0	2

THE WOMEN'S HOCKEY ASSOCIATION

1. A total of six matches would be played, and therefore a total of twelve points awarded. Since the Angels, Belles, and Colleens totaled nine points, the Dames must have had three. Since they scored no goals, they must have played three 0–0 ties.
2. The available information can be placed into the following table (the Belles have five points, which means they had to win two and tie one):

Team	*Games*	*Won*	*Lost*	*Tied*	*Goals For*	*Goals Against*	*Points*
Angels	3						1
Belles	3	2	0	1	4		5
Colleens	3					3	3
Dames	3	0	0	3	0	0	3

3. The Colleens defeated the Angels 3–2, which means the Colleens scored at least three goals and the Angels at least two. Adding these goals to the four known to be scored by the Belles gives nine, and since only nine goals were scored during the season, we know the Angels and Colleens score no goals in their other games.
4. The Colleens, with a 0–0 tie with the Dames, must have a win to earn three points. This win, we know, is over the Angels 3–2. Their third game must be a loss to the Belles, which must be 0–1, since only three goals were scored against them during the season.
5. The Belles, then, had a 0–0 tie with the Dames, and a 1–0 win over the Colleens. The Belles must have scored three goals when they played the Angels, and the Angels could not have scored any.

Answer: Belles 3, Angels 0

THE JUNGLE HOCKEY LEAGUE

1. There must be a mistake in the number of games played. The games add up to fifteen, but they must add up to an even number.
2. There must be a mistake in points: they add up to thirteen, but they must be an even number.
3. We have located two mistakes, therefore all other columns are entirely correct.

4. D, with two ties, must have two or four points; this locates the error in the points column. Two points can't be correct, since that yields a total of twelve, which is impossible with only one error in the games column (we have evidence that all teams have played at least one game, and four of the five have played three). Therefore, D must have one win, two ties, four points; win is 1–0, ties are both 0–0.

5. A has one point, so has a 0–0 tie and a loss 0–1. A's game total must be two, not three, since goals for and against do not allow for another win or loss, and points do not allow for another tie.

6. B did not have two ties, therefore B had to have two wins to earn four points. Their other game must have been a loss 0–1. Two wins had to be 2–0 and 1–0, and the 2–0 win was over E, since we are told B and E had the high scoring game.

7. C has three points with only one goal scored. They must have won 1–0, tied 0–0, and lost their third game, which must have been 0–1, since E and B had the highest scoring match (2–0).

8. Team E must have one win to earn two points, therefore two losses. One of the losses was 0–2 to B; the other must be 0–1. Given that A and E have played, and A has no wins, E must have beaten A 1–0.

9. We can now fill in the table with the above information:

	Games	Won	Lost	Tied	Goals For	Goals Against	Points
A	2	0	1	1	0	1	1
B	3	2	1	0	3	1	4
C	3	1	1	1	1	1	3
D	3	1	0	2	1	0	4
E	3	1	2	0	1	3	2

10. D's two ties have to be with A and C. Since we are given that D has played B, their win must be 1–0 over B.

11. This leaves C with a 1–0 win and a 0–1 loss. B has a 1–0 win, and E a 0–1 loss. B and E have already played, therefore E's loss must be to C, and B's win is over C.

Answer:

		Contestants			
Game	A	B	C	D	E
1	0	. . .	. . .	0	. . .
2	0	. . .	. . .	. . .	1
3	. . .	1	0	. . .	. . .
4	. . .	. . .	0	0	. . .
5	. . .	. . .	1	. . .	0
6	. . .	0	. . .	1	. . .
7	. . .	2	. . .	. . .	0

DUST BOWL HOCKEY

1. The Sidewinders' record is incorrectly listed in the *Sand Sentinel*: we know they won a match 2–1 and must have scored at least two goals. Therefore their record is correct in the *Daily Dust*.
2. The Asps' record is wrong in the *Dust*—you can't lose two games and have only one goal scored against you. The record is correct in the *Sentinel*.
3. *If* the Rattlers' record is correct in the *Dust*, the Asps, Rattlers, and Sidewinders have eight wins and three losses. The Boas, Cobras, and Pythons have at most six losses (with four wins). It is impossible to balance wins and losses, so the Rattlers must be incorrectly recorded in the *Dust*, correctly in the *Sentinel*.
4. The Asps and Rattlers are recorded correctly in the *Sentinel*. If the Boas are the third team the *Sentinel* reports accurately, then we can make up the following table:

Team	Won	Lost	Tied
Asps	4	0	1
Boas	3	1	1
Cobras	0	3	1
Pythons	2	1	0
Rattlers	1	1	3
Sidewinders	1	3	1

The table indicates eleven wins and nine losses, which is impossible. Therefore the Boas cannot be the third team correctly reported by the *Sentinel*.

5. With the Asps and Rattlers correct in the *Sentinel*, and the Boas and Sidewinders correct in the *Dust*, we have eight wins and six losses. In order to balance wins and losses, Cobras will have to be correct in the *Dust* and Pythons correct in the *Sentinel*. Thus:

Team	Games	Won	Lost	Tied	Goals For	Goals Against
Asps	5	4	0	1	5	0
Boas	4	2	2	0	2	3
Cobras	4	0	3	1	1	4
Pythons	3	2	1	0	4	1
Rattlers	5	1	1	3	1	1
Sidewinders	5	$\frac{1}{10}$	$\frac{3}{10}$	$\frac{1}{6}$	$\frac{2}{15}$	$\frac{6}{15}$

6. We know the Sidewinders win 2–1, therefore they must tie 0–0 and lose three—either 0–3, 0–1, and 0–1, or 0–2, 0–2, and 0–1.

7. The Rattlers must win 1–0, lose 0–1, and have three 0–0 ties (with the Asps, Cobras, and the Sidewinders).
8. The Cobras, with a 0–0 tie, must lose 1–2, 0–1, and 0–1, and must play the Asps, Rattlers, and Sidewinders (since they have played all five of their games).
9. The Asps must win once 2–0 and three times 1–0. Therefore their game with the Cobras is a 1–0 win.
10. But the Boas must win 1–0 twice and lose 0–1 and 0–2.
11. The Cobras have a loss to the Sidewinders. The Sidewinders have only one win, therefore the score was 2–1 (see step 6).
12. The Pythons' only loss has to be 0–1. The Asps must have played them (since they have played all five of their games). Therefore the Asps, with only wins, must have won 1–0.
13. The Pythons, then, had to win games with the Rattlers and the Sidewinders (who have also played five), so they must have beaten the Rattlers 1–0 and therefore defeated the Sidewinders 3–0 (to get a total of four goals).
14. The Sidewinders' other losses must both be 0–1 and must be to the Asps and the Boas (see step 6).
15. The Asps, then, must have a 2–0 win over the Boas—all their other games are accounted for.
16. Similarly, the Rattlers' last game must be the 1–0 win and it must be over the Boas.
17. Finally, the Boas' remaining game is the 1–0 win, and it must account for the Cobras' 0–1 loss.

Answer:

			Contestants			
Game	Asps	Boas	Cobras	Pythons	Rattlers	Sidewinders
1	2	0	. . .	. . .	. . .	. . .
2	1	. . .	0	. . .	. . .	. . .
3	1	. . .	. . .	0	. . .	. . .
4	0	. . .	. . .	. . .	0	. . .
5	1	. . .	. . .	. . .	. . .	0
6	. . .	1	0	. . .	. . .	. . .
7	. . .	0	. . .	. . .	1	. . .
8	. . .	1	. . .	. . .	. . .	0
9	. . .	. . .	0	. . .	0	. . .
10	. . .	. . .	1	. . .	. . .	2
11	. . .	. . .	. . .	1	0	. . .
12	. . .	. . .	. . .	3	. . .	0
13	. . .	. . .	. . .	. . .	0	0

A MONSTROUS HOCKEY PROBLEM

1. The Goats are incorrectly recorded in the *Potion Press*—you can't win two with only one goal scored. Therefore the Goats are correctly recorded in the *Ghoul's Gazette*.

2. The Lizards are incorrectly recorded in the *Press*—they can't have played five with a game next week. Therefore they are correctly recorded in the *Gazette*.

3. The third team that is correctly recorded in the *Gazette* could be the Alligators, the Bats, the Crocodiles, or the Dragons (the three that are not correct in the *Gazette* are correct in the *Press*).

   A. If the Alligators are correctly recorded in the *Gazette*, then there would be a total of eleven wins and seven losses. Thus we can conclude the Alligators are incorrectly recorded in the *Gazette*.

   B. If the *Gazette* records the Bats correctly, there would be a total of eight wins and eight losses. This is possible.

   C. If the Crocodiles are correctly recorded in the *Gazette*, there would be a total of seven wins and seven losses. This is possible.

   D. If the *Gazette* correctly records the Dragons, there would be a total of thirteen wins and five losses. This is impossible.

4. If the Crocodiles are correct in the *Gazette*, and the Alligators, Bats, and the Dragons are correct in the *Press*, then:

Team	Games	Won	Lost	Tied	Goals For	Goals Against
Alligators	2	0	1	1	2	3
Bats	5	2	2	1	2	4
Crocodiles	4	0	2	2	1	4
Dragons	4	1	2	1	2	5
Goats	4	1	0	3	4	2
Lizards	3	3	0	0	4	1
	$\overline{22}$	$\overline{7}$	$\overline{7}$	$\overline{8}$	$\overline{15}$	$\overline{19}$

Therefore the Crocodiles cannot be correct in the *Gazette*; the Bats must be.

5. If the Bats are correct:

Team	Games	Won	Lost	Tied	Goals For	Goals Against
Alligators	2	0	1	1	2	3
Bats	4	0	4	0	0	6
Crocodiles	5	3	1	1	6	1
Dragons	4	1	2	1	2	5
Goats	4	1	0	3	4	2
Lizards	3	3	0	0	4	1
	$\overline{22}$	$\overline{8}$	$\overline{8}$	$\overline{6}$	$\overline{18}$	$\overline{18}$

6. The Alligators, then, lose 0–1 and tie 2–2. The tie must have been with the Goats.
7. Therefore the Goats have a 2–2 tie and two 0–0 ties (with the Crocodiles and the Dragons). The Goats have a 2–0 win over the Bats or the Lizards—it must be over the Bats.
8. The Crocodiles have a tie with the Goats and a 0–1 loss. Since the Lizards have no losses, the Goats' loss must be to them. Therefore the Crocodiles' three wins are over the Alligators, the Bats, and the Dragons. The victory over the Alligators has to be a 1–0 game (see step 6). To have a total of six goals, the Crocodiles' other wins must be 4–0 and 1–0 or 3–0 and 2–0.
9. The Bats haven't played the Alligators, so they must have played the Crocodiles, Dragons, and Lizards. The losses were 0–2, 0–1, and 0–1.
10. Similarly, the Lizards haven't played the Alligators or the Goats, so they have played the Bats and the Dragons, beating one of them 2–1. The loser must have been the Dragons, since the Bats have no goals. Therefore the Lizards' other game is a 1–0 win.
11. Since the Dragons score a goal when they lose, their win has to be 1–0, and it had to have been over the Bats (because the Crocodiles' only loss is to the Lizards).
12. The Bats' last game is with the Crocodiles, then, and they must have lost 0–2.
13. The Crocodiles' last game is with the Dragons, then, and they must have won 3–0.

Answer:

Game	*Alligators*	*Bats*	*Crocodiles*	*Dragons*	*Goats*	*Lizards*
1	0	. . .	1	. . .	. . .	. . .
2	2	. . .	. . .	. . .	2	. . .
3	. . .	0	2	. . .	. . .	. . .
4	. . .	0	. . .	1	. . .	. . .
5	. . .	0	. . .	. . .	2	. . .
6	. . .	0	. . .	. . .	. . .	1
7	. . .	. . .	3	0	. . .	. . .
8	. . .	. . .	0	. . .	0	. . .
9	. . .	. . .	0	. . .	. . .	1
10	. . .	. . .	. . .	0	0	. . .
11	. . .	. . .	. . .	1	. . .	2

The big game, then, is the match between the Goats and the Lizards. If the Goats win, they tie the Crocodiles for the championship. If the Lizards win, they are the champions. In case of a tie, the Lizards and the Crocodiles would finish tied for first.

SLOBBOVIAN HOCKEY

1. In the *Dillon Daily Snowball* the Dogs are incorrectly reported—you can't lose two if only one goal has been scored against you. The Dogs' record is wrong in the *Ghastly Gazette* too: with three games played, there cannot be results for five games. Therefore the correct record for the Dogs is in the *Frozen Free Press*.

2. The Condors are wrong in the *Press*: three games, four results. The Apes are wrong in the *Gazette*: if you have a loss, you can't score a total of as many goals as you yield without getting a win.

3. Since I have a ticket for a game between the Elks and the Fangs, neither team could have finished its season. Therefore the *Press* is wrong about the Fangs, and the *Gazette* is wrong about the Elks.

4. Since both the *Snowball* and the *Press* show no ties for the Fangs, both papers must be wrong. Thus the *Gazette* has the correct season record for the Fangs.

5. By elimination, the *Press* must be right about the Dogs and the *Gazette* about the Fangs.

6. The *Gazette* must also be right about either the Bulls or the Condors. If it is right about the Bulls, then the *Snowball* has to be right about either the Apes and the Condors, the Apes and the Elks, or the Condors and the Elks.

   A. If the *Snowball* is right about the Apes and Condors, then the *Press* must have the correct record for the Elks:

Team	Games	Won	Lost	Tied
Apes	5	2	0	3
Bulls	5	2	2	1
Condors	5	2	2	1
Dogs	4	1	3	0
Elks	3	2	1	0
Fangs	3	1	1	1
		10	9	6

   Since the number of wins does not equal the number of losses, the *Press* could not have the correct record for the Elks.

   B. If the Apes and Elks are listed correctly in the *Snowball*, then the Condors must be right in the *Press*:

Team	Games	Won	Lost	Tied
Apes	5	2	0	3
Bulls	5	2	2	1
Condors	3	3	1	0
Dogs	4	1	3	0
Elks	4	1	2	1
Fangs	3	1	1	1
		10	9	6

   Wins and losses are not equal, which is impossible.

C. If the Condors and the Elks are correct in the *Snowball*, then the Apes must be right in the *Press*:

Team	Games	Won	Lost	Tied
Apes	4	1	2	1
Bulls	5	2	2	1
Condors	5	2	2	1
Dogs	4	1	3	0
Elks	4	1	3	0
Fangs	3	$\frac{1}{8}$	$\frac{1}{12}$	$\frac{1}{5}$

Again, this is clearly impossible. Since all options are unworkable if the *Gazette* is right about the Bulls, we can conclude that the *Gazette* must be wrong about the Bulls and therefore right about the Condors.

7. Since the *Gazette* is right about the Condors, the *Snowball* is right about either the Apes and the Bulls, the Apes and the Elks, or the Bulls and the Elks.

A. If the *Snowball* is right about the Apes and Bulls:

Team	Games	Won	Lost	Tied
Apes	5	2	0	3
Bulls	3	3	0	0
Condors	4	1	0	3
Dogs	4	1	3	0
Elks	3	2	1	0
Fangs	3	$\frac{1}{10}$	$\frac{1}{5}$	$\frac{1}{7}$

This is clearly impossible.

B. If the *Snowball* is right about the Apes and Elks:

Team	Games	Won	Lost	Tied	Goals For	Goals Against
Apes	5	2	0	3	3	1
Bulls	4	1	1	2	4	4
Condors	4	1	0	3	2	1
Dogs	4	1	3	0	2	5
Elks	4	1	2	1	3	3
Fangs	3	$\frac{1}{7}$	$\frac{1}{7}$	$\frac{1}{10}$	$\frac{1}{15}$	$\frac{4}{18}$

A comparison of the goals scored for and against shows that the *Snowball* could not have been right about the Apes and Elks.

C. Therefore the *Snowball* must be right about the Bulls and Elks:

Team	Games	Won	Lost	Tied	Goals For	Goals Against
Apes	4	1	2	1	1	2
Bulls	3	3	0	0	7	1
Condors	4	1	0	3	2	1
Dogs	4	1	3	0	2	5
Elks	4	1	2	1	3	3
Fangs	3	$\frac{1}{8}$	$\frac{1}{8}$	$\frac{1}{6}$	$\frac{1}{16}$	$\frac{4}{16}$

These are the true records. Now it remains to be determined who has played whom and what the scores were.

8. A. The Condors have three ties, so they must have tied the Apes, Elks, and Fangs. The Condors also have a 1–0 win, which must have been over the Dogs, since the Bulls, the other possibility, have no losses.

   B. The Apes have a 1–0 win, so their tie with the Condors must have been 0–0.

   C. The Fangs must have a 1–0 win—the only possibility, since they have scored only one goal. They also must have tied the Condors 0–0.

   D. By elimination, the Elks and Condors must have tied 1–1. We know all of the Condors' scores now.

9. If the Fangs have a 1–0 win and a 0–0 tie, their third game has to be a 0–4 loss.

10. The Fangs' loss must have been to the Bulls, since nobody else could have scored four times in one game. The Bulls' other two wins, then, had to be 2–1 and 1–0.

11. Since the Elks played a 1–1 tie, both of their losses had to have been 0–1, and their one win had to be 2–0.

12. The Apes must have won 1–0 and lost two games 0–1.

13. Since all other scores are now determined, the Bulls' 2–1 victory has to be over the Dogs. The Dogs' other games have to be the 0–1 loss to the Condors, a 1–0 victory, and a 0–2 loss (which must be the game the Elks won).

14. By examining all the results we have determined thus far, we can conclude that the only team the Apes could have beaten 1–0 was the Elks.

15. We still need to determine which teams played in the outstanding 1–0 matches. The Bulls, Dogs, and Fangs have 1–0 wins; the Elks have a 0–1 loss and the Apes have two 0–1 losses. The Dogs' win is not over the Elks (they have already met), so it must be over the Apes. Either the Dogs or the Fangs have a 1–0 win over the Elks, but

we know from the second sentence of the problem that the Elks and
Fangs are to play next week. Therefore the Elks lost to the Dogs 0–1
and the Fangs' 1–0 win was over the Apes.

Answer:

	Contestants					
Game	Apes	Bulls	Condors	Dogs	Elks	Fangs
1	0	. . .	0	. . .	. . .	. . .
2	0	. . .	. . .	1	. . .	. . .
3	1	. . .	. . .	. . .	0	. . .
4	0	. . .	. . .	. . .	. . .	1
5	. . .	2	. . .	1	. . .	. . .
6	. . .	1	. . .	. . .	0	. . .
7	. . .	4	. . .	. . .	. . .	0
8	. . .	. . .	1	0	. . .	. . .
9	. . .	. . .	1	. . .	1	. . .
10	. . .	. . .	0	. . .	. . .	0
11	. . .	. . .	. . .	0	2	. . .

ALL THE NEWS THAT'S FIT TO PRINT

1. Sixteen points scored means there were eight games played. Each
   team plays four during the season, for a total of ten games. Therefore
   two games are yet to be played.
2. From the column totals we can see that of the eight games played
   there were four wins and four ties.
3. Since two games remain to be played, each team must have played
   at least two. So the Apes and the Braves have played two or three
   games (since a total of four games for each team is wrong). The
   Chiefs and Eagles have played two or four, and the Devils have
   played three or four.
4. We know the Chiefs and Eagles played to a tie, but since one is the
   wrong total of ties for the Chiefs, the Chiefs must have at least two
   ties. We are given that the Chiefs have played one match that was not
   a tie; we know they have played two or four games: therefore they
   have exactly two ties and either two wins or two losses.
5. Wherever a zero appears, the true answer must be one or higher.
   The Eagles, then, have at least one win and one tie and have played
   two or four games. They can't have three ties because that would
   give them five points. Therefore the Eagles must have one tie.
6. The Apes have at least one win, but they can't have two ties. Therefore
   the maximum number of ties for the Apes is one.

7. The Braves have at least one loss and cannot have two ties. Therefore they must have at most one tie.
8. The maximum number of ties for the Apes, Braves, Chiefs, and Eagles is five. Since the total number of points from ties is eight, the Devils must have three (they couldn't have four—we know the Chiefs or Eagles had one of the four).
9. We now know this much about the standings:

Team	Games	Won	Lost	Tied	Points
Apes	2 or 3			1	
Braves	2 or 3			1	
Chiefs	2 or 4			2	
Devils	4	0	1	3	3
Eagles	2 or 4			1	

10. The Apes and Braves have not completed their schedules: each must have at least one game to go. They can't both have two games to play, since that would require them to play each other twice. Similarly, one of them can't have two games to play and the other one game, since that would require another team to have only one game to play, and no other team has just one game left to play. Therefore the Apes and Braves have played three games each, and either the Chiefs or the Eagles still have two games to play, one with the Apes and one with the Braves.
11. Since we know the Chiefs and Eagles tied, the other ties are between the Devils and Apes, the Devils and Braves, and the Devils and Chiefs. The Devils' other match must have been a loss to the Eagles.
12. Now we know that the Eagles beat the Devils and tied the Chiefs. Either the Eagles have not yet played the Apes and Braves, or they have played them both. Since the Eagles could not have just one loss or a total of five points, if they played the Apes and Braves they had either to win both or lose both games.
13. We know the Chiefs had one match that was not a tie, so the Chiefs, since they could not have just one loss or a total of four points, either beat both the Apes and Braves or lost to both.
14. We know from step 12 that the Eagles either defeated the Apes and Braves, lost to both, or have yet to play both. If the Eagles defeated the Apes and Braves, however, then the Chiefs have played only two games, both of which were ties; but I saw the Chiefs play a game that was not a tie. So the Eagles must be the team that has not yet played the Apes and Braves.
15. We know from step 13 that the Chiefs either beat both the Apes and Braves or lost to both.
    A. Assume the Chiefs defeat both the Apes and Braves (the Apes, then, must have beaten the Braves in order for them not to have finished with two losses):

Team	Games	Won	Lost	Tied	Points
Apes	3	1	1	1	3
Braves	3	0	2	1	1
Chiefs	4	2	0	2	6
Devils	4	0	1	3	3
Eagles	2	1	0	1	3

  B. This gives the Apes three points, however, which violates given conditions. Therefore the Chiefs could not have won two.
16. The Chiefs, then, must have lost to both the Apes and Braves, and the Apes must have beaten the Braves, depriving the Braves of a second win.

Answer:

Team	Games	Won	Lost	Tied	Points
Apes	3	2	0	1	5
Braves	3	1	1	1	3
Chiefs	4	0	2	2	2
Devils	4	0	1	3	3
Eagles	2	1	0	1	3

Remaining games: Apes versus Eagles and Braves versus Eagles.

ALL GREEK

1. A. Argo cannot be reported correctly in the *Spartan Sentinel*—with two ties and two losses it is not possible to have only one more goal scored against than for.
   B. For similar reasons, Boeotia cannot be reported correctly in the *Peloponnesian Press*.
   C. Similarly, Delphi is incorrectly reported in the *Press*—you can't win two with just one goal.
2. One of the five teams is reported incorrectly on every figure in both papers. Since a maximum of four games were played by each team, knowing two wrong figures leaves us the possible right figures. Therefore let us test each team to see if it was the one reported incorrectly by both papers.

Team	Games	Won	Lost	Tied
Argo	0, 1, or 2	1	1	0
Boeotia	0, 1, or 2	1	1 or 2	1
Corinth	1 or 4	1 or 3	2 or 3	1 or 3

Team	Games	Won	Lost	Tied
Delphi	0, 1, or 2	0	0	1 or 2
Epirus	0, 1, or 2	0	1 or 2	2

Boeotia and Epirus could not have been incorrectly reported by both papers for the same reason: they both would have had to play a minimum of three games in order to accommodate their record of wins, losses, and ties. Therefore at this point we can see that either Argo, Corinth, or Delphi could be the team that is wrong in both papers.

3. A. Let's assume Argo is wrong in both papers. Then we know Boeotia and Delphi's true records and can generate the following table:

Team	Games	Won	Lost	Tied
Argo	2	1	1	0
Boeotia	4	2	0	2
Corinth				2 or 0
Delphi	3	1	2	0
Epirus				1 or 0

Since Corinth and Epirus are both right in one paper or the other, Corinth has two or no ties and Epirus has one or none. But it is impossible for Corinth to have two ties if Epirus has one, since this would yield an odd number of ties, and you can only have a tie if two teams each get one. It is also impossible for Corinth to have two if Epirus has none, since Boeotia and Corinth play each other only once. Furthermore, it is impossible for Corinth to have no ties, since Boeotia would have two and there is a maximum of only one for the rest of the league combined. We can conclude, therefore, that Argo is not the team that is incorrectly reported in both papers and, hence, Argo must be correct in the *Press*.

B. Assume Delphi is wrong in both papers:

Team	Games	Won	Lost	Tied
Argo	3	2	0	1
Boeotia	4	2	0	2
Corinth	2 or 3	2 or 0	0 or 1	0 or 2
Delphi	0, 1, or 2	0	0	1 or 2
Epirus	3 or 4	2 or 1	0 or 3	1 or 0

Since this distribution shows a minimum of five wins and a maximum of four losses, it cannot be correct. Therefore Delphi is not incorrectly reported in both papers and, hence, is correct in the *Sentinel*.

C. Therefore Corinth must be the team that is wrong in both papers:

Team	Games	Won	Lost	Tied	Goals For	Goals Against
Argo	3	2	0	1	2	0
Boeotia	4	2	0	2	3	0
Corinth	1 or 4	1 or 3	2 or 3	1 or 3		
Delphi	3	1	2	0	2	4
Epirus I	4	1	3	0	2	3
Epirus II	3	2	0	1	4	4

(The two entries for Epirus reflect that team's possible records at this point in our deduction.)

4. Examining the distribution in step 3C above, which is based on the assumption that Corinth is wrong in both papers, we can conclude the following:

   A. Corinth has one tie or three. Either way Epirus must have none (to yield an even number). Thus we know that Epirus must be correctly listed in the *Press*.

   B. It is impossible for Corinth to have three ties, since they would have to play Boeotia twice. Therefore Corinth has one tie.

   C. Corinth must have played four games, since one game is impossible if a team has wins, losses, and a tie.

   D. Corinth cannot have three wins, since that would require them to have played more than four games. Corinth therefore has played four, won one, lost two, and tied one.

   E. Now let's consider goals for and against Corinth. In light of its won–lost record, Corinth must have two more goals scored against than for. Since the number of goals cannot be two or three, it must be one, four, or more than four. Correspondingly, goals against would be three, six, or more than six.

   F. Epirus lost three games, yielding a total of three goals; therefore the scores had to have been 0–1, 0–1, and 0–1. Epirus won a game 2–0.

   G. Boeotia has two ties. Since the team did not yield any goals, both ties had to be 0–0. Boeotia therefore won games by 1–0 and 2–0.

   H. Argo tied Boeotia 0–0 and had two 1–0 wins. Thus we know these records:

	Contestants				
Game	*Argo*	*Boeotia*	*Corinth*	*Delphi*	*Epirus*	*Unknown*
1	0	0	. . .	. . .	. . .	. . .
2	1	. . .	. . .	. . .	. . .	0
3	1	. . .	. . .	. . .	. . .	0
4	. . .	0	0	. . .	. . .	. . .

	Contestants					
Game	Argo	Boeotia	Corinth	Delphi	Epirus	Unknown
5	. . .	2	. . .	. . .	. . .	0
6	. . .	1	. . .	. . .	. . .	0
7	. . .	. . .	. . .	. . .	2	0
8	. . .	. . .	. . .	. . .	0	1
9	. . .	. . .	. . .	. . .	0	1
10	. . .	. . .	. . .	. . .	0	1

(Note that the total number of games at this point may be incorrect since we have not yet identified the contestants for each game.)

I. Since Epirus has played all its games, Argo and Boeotia must have each beaten Epirus (they have no losses), and those wins must both have been 1–0. Boeotia had ties with Argo and Corinth, so their 2–0 win had to be over Delphi.

J. Argo, Boeotia, and Corinth all have both ties and games that did not end in ties on their record. Therefore they cannot be the team that had every match end with an identical score. We know that Epirus was involved in 1–0 and 0–2 matches. Therefore Delphi must be the team, and all Delphi's games must have ended in 2–0 scores (one win and two losses). Epirus' 2–0 game must have been a win over Delphi, and Delphi therefore had to defeat Corinth 2–0.

Answer:

	Contestants				
Game	Argo	Boeotia	Corinth	Delphi	Epirus
1	0	0	. . .	. . .	. . .
2	1	. . .	0	. . .	. . .
3	1	. . .	. . .	. . .	0
4	. . .	0	0	. . .	. . .
5	. . .	2	. . .	0	. . .
6	. . .	1	. . .	. . .	0
7	. . .	. . .	0	2	. . .
8	. . .	. . .	1	. . .	0
9	. . .	. . .	. . .	0	2

Solutions to Seven Days of Racing

MONDAY

1. Since every secretary won a different number of races, they must have won five, four, three, two, and one in some order, or a total of fifteen.
2. For Queenie to win twice as many races as Tess, she must have won an even number, either two or four. Since she knows she is ahead of one other person, she must have four winners rather than two.
3. One secretary picked five winners—four the same as Queenie and one different. Pat has three choices different from Queenie, and so does Rhoda, so neither one could have five winners; nor does Tess, who has only two.
4. Sal, then, must have five winners.

Answer:
Ariana, Beowulf, Cedric, Derek, and Fizz are the winning horses. Sal is the most successful secretary.

TUESDAY

1. With one secretary picking one winner more, another picking one winner fewer, than the other three, the distribution of winners could be five, four, four, four, and three; four, three, three, three, and two; or three, two, two, two, and one. If the "favorite" won each race, a maximum of thirteen winners is possible, which rules out the first two distributions. Therefore we know the number of winners picked was three, two, two, two, and one.
2. Three women picked the same horse in three races. Since we are given that most of the women picked the winner together for only one race, only one of the three horses picked in common could have been a winner.
   A. If three women picked the winner for the fifth race, and we add the maximum number of winners for the other four races, we get a maximum total number of winners of nine. Since we know that there were ten winners, Vandal must have lost the fifth race. (Vesper must have won.)
   B. Since no one who won on the fifth race also won on the second, Ronin and Rancho both lost the second race. That leaves Ribald as the winner, picked by three women. It follows that Tornado lost the fourth race, since the majority of the women won only one race together. Thus the required distribution of winning bets by race is two, three, two, one, and two.
   C. Therefore horses picked by only one secretary in the first and third races (Peony and Saki respectively) must have lost.
   D. Either Picardy or Pocono won the first race. If Picardy won, then either Donna (who bet on Samurai in the third) or Greta (who bet on Shogun in the third) would have to have won on both races. Since we know nobody won on both races, Picardy must have lost the first race and Pocono won it.

E. Since Pocono won the first race and no woman won on both the first and the third, Shogun must have lost the third race and Samurai won it.
F. We now know the winners of four races. For the fourth race, however, either Toggle or Tempest could have won. If Tempest won, each secretary would have picked exactly two winners. Therefore Toggle must have won, and Eva picked three winners while Greta picked only one.

Answer:
The horses are Pocono, Ribald, Samurai, Toggle, and Vesper. Eva picked three winners.

WEDNESDAY

1. Warlord could not have won the sixth race, since the women who bet on him also chose all three of the listed horses for the fifth: someone would have won twice in a row.
2. Therefore Whisper won the sixth (we are given that Wompus lost, and know from step 1 that Warlord lost).
3. Since nobody won twice in a row, we know that Yellow and Yonder both lost the seventh (so Yolande won).
4. Since nobody won twice in a row, we know that Vasco lost the fifth.
5. Since nobody won twice in a row, we know that Zither and Zig-Zag must have lost the eighth (so Zebulon must have won).
6. Since no two persons won together twice, Tidal must have lost the third race (because Cassie and Ella both bet on Tidal, and both won together in the seventh race).
7. With a total of five winners in races 6, 7, and 8, and at least one in the other three races, there had to be at least eight total winners, and at most fifteen. Since all six women picked the same number of winners, each must have won just twice, for a total of twelve winners.
8. It has been established above that Cassie lost on the third, fifth, sixth, and eighth races, and won on the seventh. From step 7 we know she picked two winners, therefore she must have won the fourth, and Uranus was the winning horse.
9. If Uranus won the fourth, Vibrate had to lose in the fifth and Twist had to lose in the first to satisfy the condition that nobody won twice in a row. Therefore we know Trump won the first race and Victor won the third.

Answer:
Trump, Uranus, Victor, Whisper, Yolande, and Zebulon are the winners.

THURSDAY

1. Because Gloria never won when Ida did, we know that Coyote lost the third race, Fuller B lost the sixth, and Gem lost the seventh.
2. Because Hattie never won when Jean did, we know Bourbon lost the second race, Evasion the fifth, and Hideout the eighth.

3. Dibs cannot have won the fourth race, since the women who bet on Dibs also bet on both remaining possibilities in the fifth, and nobody won twice in a row.
4. Now we can tabulate the number of possible winners for each race:

			Race				

	First	*Second*	*Third*	*Fourth*	*Fifth*	*Sixth*	*Seventh*	*Eighth*
Winning bets	1 or 3	1 or 2	1 or 2	1 or 2	2	2 or 3	1 or 3	2

There is thus a minimum of eleven winning bets and a maximum of nineteen. With six women tied for the number of winners, and one woman two wins ahead, the possibilities are:

A. Six women tied with one win each: total of nine winners;
B. Six women tied with two wins each: total of sixteen winners;
C. Six women tied with three wins each: total of twenty-three winners.

Possibility B lies within the minimum-maximum range.

Considering the horses we have established as losers, every woman but one has lost in both odd- and even-numbered races. The woman who won four races won either all odd-numbered or all even-numbered races—it must have been Laura who won the odd races.

5. Laura lost the even-numbered races, so we know Bon-Bon and Foamy are losers. Since Mona won on the seventh with Laura, Happy must have lost the eighth.
6. In order for each woman to have two wins, Blondie had to win the second and Dogma the fourth.

Answer:
The horses are Alpha, Blondie, Cygnus, Dogma, Erewhon, Firefly, Gilda, and Haircut. Laura won four races.

FRIDAY

1. For five people each to have the same number of winners, the total number of winners must be a multiple of five—five, ten, fifteen, etc. In two of the races most of the women—meaning three or four out of five—picked winners, thus there was a minimum of six winners for these two races. For each of the other six races, there was a minimum of one winning bet. Therefore the minimum number of winners for the afternoon is twelve. The maximum number is eighteen—two winners for each of six races, and three winners for two races (on no race did four women bet on the same horse, so "most" in the problem must mean three). Thus the total number of winners is fifteen.
2. Three women picked the same horse in races 2, 5, and 7, but the majority was right only twice. Since no two women won together more than once, the two races for which the majority of women picked the winner cannot be 2 and 7 because Sarah and Trixie picked the same horse both times. Thus the two races must be either 2 and 5 or 7 and 5. Either way, Kinky must have won the fifth race. Miracle, then, must have lost the seventh, since Sarah and Wanda both bet on Kinky in the

fifth and Miracle in the seventh. Therefore Miser won the seventh, and we can conclude that Handy, the favorite, won the second.

3. Applying the principle that no two women won together twice, we can determine:
   A. Since Handy won the second, Gamin lost the first, Narrows lost the eighth, and Ironize lost the third.
   B. Since Kinky won the fifth, Gorilla lost the first. Garland, then, must have won the first and Lola lost the sixth.
4. We now have three winners for Sarah (races 1, 2, and 5). Therefore Sarah must have lost on races 3, 4, 6, 7, and 8.
5. Since Miser won the seventh, Linkage must have lost the sixth, since Una and Violet bet on both. Laser therefore won the sixth.
6. At this point the distribution of winners by race is:

Race

	First	Second	Third	Fourth	Fifth	Sixth	Seventh	Eighth
Winners	1	3	1 or 2	1 or 2	3	1	2	1 or 2

The minimum number of winners in the distribution is thirteen, the maximum is sixteen. We know we have to come out with fifteen winners total, therefore five winners must be found for the three races for which the winners are unknown. Therefore in two of the three races, a horse with two bets on it must have won. The possibilities are:
   A. The third and eighth races; but this possibility can be ruled out, since Trixie and Wanda backed the same horses.
   B. Races 3 and 4.
   C. Races 4 and 8.
Whether the answer is possibility B or C, Jutland must have won the fourth race.

7. Either the third or the eighth race was won by two women.
   A. If two women bet on the winner in the third, Ideal won, and Nick-Nack won the eighth. This yields no winner of just odd- or even-numbered races, however, and must be rejected.
   B. If two women picked the winner in the eighth, the winner was Nuisance—the third winner for Trixie and Wanda. Ignition is Una's third winning bet. Una wins the third, fifth, and seventh; Trixie wins the second, sixth, and eighth.

Answer:
The winning horses are Garland, Handy, Ignition, Jutland, Kinky, Laser, Miser, and Nuisance.

SATURDAY

1. Cathy and Ellie never both pick the winner, so Finian, Goodbar, and Hopeful must have lost.
2. Dottie and Francie never both pick a winner, so Aces, Corky, and Gesture must have lost.
3. Annie and Dotty never both pick a winner, so Elfin must have lost.

4. We are given that Edgy lost the fifth, so Easier must have won it. Furthermore we can deduce from steps 1 and 2 that Gala won the seventh.
5. At this point the possible number of winners by race is:

Race

	First	Second	Third	Fourth	Fifth	Sixth	Seventh	Eighth
Winners	1 or 2	1 or 3	1 or 3	1 or 3	2	1 or 2	1	1

The minimum number of possible winners is nine, the maximum is seventeen. For all but one secretary to have the same number of winners, the total number of winners picked has to be seven, thirteen, or nineteen. Therefore there were exactly thirteen winners.
6. Annie and Betty won together once—had to be on the second or third race.
7. Cathy and Francie won together once—had to be on the fifth race (we know Easier won). Therefore Barge lost the second.
8. Whether the race both Annie and Betty won on was the second or third, a third woman won with them, and that race must be the one for which three women picked the winner. Therefore Deft must have lost the fourth.
9. We now know Ellie lost races 4, 5, 6, 7, and 8. Since she bet with Annie and Betty in the second and third, she won one and lost one. Therefore her second win must have been in the first race, with Advance.
10. Annie and Betty won together either in the second or the third race. Assume it was the third:
    A. Then Caution lost the third, and Cathy had to have her other win in the fourth, with Dum-Dum.
    B. Then Dotty lost the fourth and had to win the second and eighth (having lost the other six races).
    C. Francie, then, lost the eighth, and had to win the sixth, with Folly.
    D. This analysis gives Annie four winners: Advance, Careful, Dum-Dum, and Folly—which violates given conditions. Thus we know Annie and Betty could not have won the third race together· they must have won the second race together.
11. It follows that Dotty had to win the fourth and eighth races. Francie, then, lost the eighth, and so had to win the sixth.

Answer:
The winning horses are Advance, Bella, Caution, Doily, Easier, Folly, Gala, and Headless. Annie won three races.

SUNDAY

1. Each secretary won the same number of races. This number cannot be one because, if it were, more than one secretary would have lost money. The number cannot be three, since even if the favorite were to win every time, there would only be twelve winners. Therefore each secretary won twice.

2. In order to win on two races and still lose money, both wins would have to be at 2–1 odds. Thus only Joan or Laura could have lost money. If the two 2–1 victories were by Whirlybird and Bolero, both Joan and Laura would have lost money; so both Whirlybird and Bolero could not have won. There are four other possibilities:
   A. Laura won on Whirlybird and Dark Prince.
   B. Laura won on Bolero and Dark Prince.
   C. Joan won with Whirlybird and Argon.
   D. Joan won with Argon and Bolero.
3. If Laura won with Whirlybird and Dark Prince (and lost on Avalanche, Bolero, and Cabal), the maximum number of winners by race is:

	First	*Second*	*Third*	*Fourth*	*Fifth*
			Race		
Winners	2	2	1	1	1

   This yields a total of seven winners, which is impossible.
4. We know we need a total of ten winners, and let's assume Laura won with Bolero and Dark Prince. What horse won the fourth race? If either Crouton or Cinnamon won, the maximum possible number of winners is nine, which we know is incorrect. If Cabal won the fourth, the total number of winners is eleven (two, two, three, three, and one winners on the first through fifth race respectively)—impossible. Therefore Laura could not have won with Bolero and Dark Prince.
5. If Joan won on Argon and Bolero, she lost on Crouton; so either Cabal or Cinnamon won the fourth race.
   A. If Cabal won, Joan, Laura, and Nell have two wins each spread over races 2, 3, and 4. Therefore, in order for no one to have three winners, Drudgery, Dark Prince, and Dirty Dingo all had to lose the fifth; but since these were the only horses that could have won the fifth, this solution is impossible.
   B. If Cinnamon won the fourth, in order to get a total of ten winners, Wagoneer must have won the first and Dirty Dingo the fifth. But that makes three winners for Nell and only one for Laura—impossible. Therefore Joan could not have won on Argon and Bolero.
6. By elimination, then, Joan must have won on Whirlybird and Argon.
   A. Therefore Bolero, Crouton, and Drudgery all lost.
   B. In order to get a total of ten winners, Cabal must have won the fourth.
   C. Laura has two winners with Whirlybird and Cabal, therefore Dark Prince must have lost and Dirty Dingo won the fifth race.
   D. Marge's second winner has to be Bedelia.
7. Joan, then, paid out $5 for each of five races plus $5 for the pool. She got back $20 on two races, $12.50 from the pool for having lost money on the five races, and $2.50 that she had put in the pool.
8. Marge bet $25, won $35, and lost $2.50 on the pool.
9. Kaye and Nell are each $2.50 ahead for the day. Laura is $2.50 behind.

Answer:
The winning horses were Whirlybird, Argon, Bedelia, Cabal, and Dirty Dingo. Marge won the most money: $7.50. Joan did second best: $5 ahead for the day.

Solutions to Six Leagues of Prophets

1993

1. Note that there are three true predictions and nine false. The team that comes in first place makes two true predictions.
2. The Mets, Cubs, and Expos could not have finished in first, since each of these teams predicts another team will finish first.
3. Assume the Cardinals finish first and thus make two true predictions. Then the partial standings would be the Cardinals in first, the Cubs in second, and the Pirates in fifth. The Cubs, finishing in second, must make a true prediction, but they are wrong about the Pirates finishing first and about the Expos finishing second. Therefore the Cardinals could not have finished in first.
4. Assume the Pirates are first and thus make two true predictions. Then the partial standings would have the Pirates in first, the Phillies in third, and the Cardinals in fourth.
   A. The Cubs made a true prediction about the Pirates, and therefore would have to be the second-place team.
   B. As the fourth-place team the Cardinals made two incorrect predictions, but they predicted the Cubs would come in second, which in this trial is true. Therefore the Cardinals could not have finished fourth, and the Pirates did not win the pennant.
5. Assume the Phillies finish in first and thus make two true predictions. Then our partial standings would have the Phillies in first, the Mets in third, and the Cubs in fifth.
   A. Both of the Mets' predictions are incorrect, so the Expos cannot be fourth. Both of the Expos' predictions are wrong, also, so the Expos must have finished sixth.
   B. The Cardinals are wrong about the Cubs and the Pirates, therefore the Cardinals had to finish fourth.
   C. The Pirates' prediction about the Cardinals, then, was true. Thus the Pirates finished second.

Answer:

Standing	Team	Standing	Team
First	Phillies	*Fourth*	Cardinals
Second	Pirates	*Fifth*	Cubs
Third	Mets	*Sixth*	Expos

1994

1. The Expos can't finish in first, since then their prediction about the Pirates would be incorrect. The Pirates can't finish in first either, since then their prediction about the Cardinals would be incorrect.
2. Let's assume that the Cardinals finish in first and that their two predictions are correct. The partial final standings, then, would have the Cardinals in first, the Expos in fifth, and the Cubs in sixth.
   A. The Pirates correctly predicted that the Cardinals would finish first, so the Pirates must have finished second or third.
   B. Both of the Cubs' predictions are incorrect, so the Phillies cannot finish third; they must have been in second or fourth.
   C. If the Phillies finish second, they had to have made one correct prediction. They are wrong about the Pirates, so they would have to be right about their other prediction, that the Mets would finish second, which is impossible. Therefore the Phillies can't be second; they must finish fourth.
   D. The Phillies, then, must be wrong about the Mets, who must have finished third.
   E. The Pirates are left in second, which violates the given condition that the Mets finish ahead of the Pirates. Therefore we can conclude that the Cardinals did not finish in first place.
3. Let's assume that the Cubs finish in first and that their two predictions are therefore correct.
   A. Therefore the Phillies finish third, which means that they must have one correct prediction. They are wrong about the Mets, so they must be right about the Pirates, who must have finished fourth.
   B. The Cubs should be correct about the Mets finishing fifth, but this would place the Pirates ahead of the Mets, which contradicts given conditions. Therefore the Cubs can't finish in first place.
4. Let's assume the Mets finish in first and make two correct predictions. That would put the Expos in third and the Phillies in fourth.
   A. The Expos must have one right prediction. They are wrong about the Pirates, so they must be right about the Cardinals, who must have finished sixth.
   B. Both of the Cubs' predictions are incorrect, so they could not have finished second; they must have finished fifth.
   C. By elimination, the Pirates finished second. But then they would have had to have one correct prediction; both of their predictions, however, are false. Therefore the Mets could not have finished in first place.
5. Assume the Phillies finished in first and made two correct predictions. That would put the Mets in second and the Pirates in fourth.
   A. Since the Mets' prediction about the Phillies is wrong, their prediction about the Expos must be right: the Expos finished third.
   B. Since the Expos are wrong about the Pirates, they must be right about the Cardinals, who must have finished sixth.
   C. The Cubs, then, must have finished fifth.

Answer:

Standing	Team	Standing	Team
First	Phillies	Fourth	Pirates
Second	Mets	Fifth	Cubs
Third	Expos	Sixth	Cardinals

1995

1. The Cubs could not have finished first, since they did not finish ahead of the Expos.
2. Suppose the Pirates finished first and thus made two correct predictions. That would put the Mets in third and the Cubs in fifth.
   A. Since we are given that the Expos did not finish second, they must have finished fourth or sixth.
   B. The Mets, in third, made two incorrect predictions. Hence the Cardinals could not have finished fourth.
   C. Both of the Cardinals' predictions were incorrect: the Mets, not the Expos, finished third, and the Pirates finished first, not fourth. Therefore the Cardinals must have finished fourth or sixth; but we know from step 2B that the Cardinals did not finish fourth, so they must have finished sixth.
   D. If the Cardinals finished sixth, from step 2A we can deduce that the Expos finished fourth.
   E. By elimination, the Phillies finished second. But we are given that the Phillies did *not* finish second. Therefore the Pirates could not have finished first.
3. Suppose the Cardinals finished first and made two correct predictions. That would put the Expos in third and the Pirates in fourth.
   A. The Mets were wrong on both of their predictions: the Cardinals did not finish fourth, and the Phillies did not finish third. With no correct predictions, the Mets must have finished fifth or sixth.
   B. The Phillies were wrong on both of their predictions, and must have finished fifth or sixth.
   C. By elimination, the Cubs must have finished second, but this violates one of the given conditions, that the Cubs did not finish ahead of the Expos. Therefore the Cardinals did not come in first place.
4. Suppose the Phillies finished first and made two correct predictions. This would put the Pirates in third and the Cardinals in sixth.
   A. Both of the Mets' predictions were wrong, so they must have finished in fourth or fifth.
   B. The Expos or the Cubs must have finished second. But we are given that the Expos did not finish second. Furthermore, if the Cubs finished second, that would contradict another given condition, that they finish ahead of the Expos. Therefore the Phillies could not have finished in first place.
5. Suppose the Mets finished in first place and made two correct

predictions. That would put the Phillies in third and the Cardinals in fourth.

A. Both of the Expos' predictions are wrong, so they must have finished in fifth or sixth.

B. By elimination, either the Cubs or the Pirates came in second.
   1. If the Cubs finished second, they would have come in ahead of the Expos—impossible.
   2. If the Pirates finished second, their one correct prediction must have been that the Cubs finished fifth, but this also would put the Cubs ahead of the Expos. Therefore the Mets could not have finished in first place.

6. Suppose the Expos finished in first and made two correct predictions. That would put the Cubs in fourth and the Cardinals in fifth.

A. We are given that the Phillies did not finish second. Therefore the Mets or Pirates had to have finished second.

B. If the Pirates finished second, their one true prediction must have been that the Mets finished third. This leaves the Expos in sixth, a violation of given conditions. Thus the Pirates could not have finished second.

C. By elimination, the Mets finished second. Their one true prediction must be that the Phillies finished third. Hence the Pirates finished sixth.

Answer:

Standing	Team	Standing	Team
First	Expos	Fourth	Cubs
Second	Mets	Fifth	Cardinals
Third	Phillies	Sixth	Pirates

1996

1. There are six pairs of predictions. Both statements of one pair are incorrect. There are five true predictions distributed among the remaining five pairs. Since only one team had two wrong predictions, each of the remaining five teams had at least one true prediction. Thus each of the five teams that did not finish in last place had one correct prediction and one incorrect prediction.

2. Consider the two predictions about sixth place. Either both of the predictions were incorrect, or one was true.

A. Assume both predictions about sixth place were wrong.
   1. Since neither the Cardinals nor the Cubs finished in sixth, neither made two wrong predictions.
   2. The Cardinals and Expos both made predictions about second and sixth. If the Cardinals did not finish sixth, one of their predictions must have been true, and it could not have been the one about the Cubs. Therefore the Phillies must have finished second.
   3. The Expos, then, were wrong on both of their predictions: the

Phillies, not the Mets, finished second, and the Cardinals did not finish sixth. With two incorrect predictions, the Expos must have finished sixth.
  B. The Phillies, then, were wrong about the Expos, so their other prediction, that the Pirates would finish third, must be true.
  C. The Pirates, then, were wrong about the Expos, and they were also wrong about the Mets—both the Pirates and the Mets could not have finished in third. Since only one team could have made two wrong predictions, however, both statements about who came in sixth place cannot be incorrect.
3. Assume, then, that the Cardinals finished sixth and that the Expos' prediction about them was true.
  A. The Cubs' prediction about the Cardinals is incorrect, so their other prediction, that the Pirates would finish first, must be true.
  B. The Phillies' prediction about the Pirates finishing third must be wrong, so their other prediction must be true: the Expos finished first. But the Expos and the Pirates both could not have finished in first place, therefore the Cardinals could not have finished sixth.
4. Assume that the Cubs finished sixth and that the Cardinals' prediction about them was correct.
  A. The Expos were therefore wrong about the Cardinals and must have been right about the Mets finishing second.
  B. The Pirates were wrong about the Mets, so they must have been right about the Expos—fifth place.
  C. The Phillies were wrong about the Expos, so they must have been right about the Pirates—third place.
  D. Since the Cubs made two wrong predictions, the Cardinals did not finish fourth. By elimination, the Cardinals must have finished first.
  E. The Mets were wrong about the Cubs, so they must have been right about the Phillies—fourth place.

Answer:

Standing	Team	Standing	Team
First	Cardinals	Fourth	Phillies
Second	Mets	Fifth	Expos
Third	Pirates	Sixth	Cubs

1997

1. Since the sixth-place team had two true predictions, it is reasonable to begin by looking for the sixth-place team.
2. The Expos could not have finished sixth and have two true predictions, since they predicted the Mets would finish sixth.
3. Similarly, the Cardinals could not have finished sixth, since they predicted the Pirates would come in last.
4. If the Pirates finished in sixth, then the Cardinals' prediction about them would be true, which would mean that the Cardinals finished

fifth. But the Pirates predicted the Expos finished fifth. We can conclude that the Pirates could not have finished sixth.

5. If the Mets finished sixth, the Expos' prediction about them is true, which would mean that the Expos finished fifth. The Pirates, then, had to finish in the top four and have two wrong predictions. But the Pirates correctly predicted that the Expos would finish fifth. Therefore the Mets could not have finished in last place.

6. If the Cubs finished sixth, the Cardinals finished fourth and the Pirates third.
   A. Both of the Mets' predictions were incorrect, so the Mets must have finished first or second.
   B. Both of the third-place Pirates' predictions were wrong, so the Expos could not have finished fifth—they must have finished first or second.
   C. By elimination, then, the Phillies must have finished in fifth and have had one true prediction, that the Mets finished second.
   D. Since we were given that the Phillies did not finish fifth, we can conclude that the Cubs could not have finished sixth.

7. By elimination, then, the Phillies must have finished sixth, which puts the Mets in second and the Cubs in fifth.
   A. The Mets must have made two incorrect predictions, so the Cardinals could not have finished in first.
   B. The Cardinals must have made two incorrect predictions, so the Expos could not have finished in first.
   C. By elimination, the Pirates finished first.
   D. The Cubs must have made one true prediction. They were wrong about the Pirates, so they must have been right about the Cardinals finishing in fourth.
   E. By elimination, the Expos finished in third.

Answer:

Standing	Team	Standing	Team
First	Pirates	*Fourth*	Cardinals
Second	Mets	*Fifth*	Cubs
Third	Expos	*Sixth*	Phillies

1998

1. Since the sixth-place team had two true predictions, it is reasonable to begin by looking for the sixth-place team.
2. The Pirates could not have finished in sixth and made two true predictions, since they predicted the Mets would finish in sixth.
3. Similarly, the Cardinals could not have finished in sixth, since they predicted the Phillies would.
4. If the Cubs finished in sixth, their two predictions would put the Mets in second and the Expos in fifth. This leaves the Phillies in one of the first four places and, hence, with two incorrect predictions. Therefore both the Mets and the Phillies were wrong about the Pirates, so the

Pirates could not have finished in first or third. By elimination, the Pirates finished fourth. But we were given that the Pirates did not finish fourth, so the Cubs could not have finished in sixth place.

5. If the Mets finished sixth, then the Pirates were first and the Cardinals fourth. The Pirates would have had to have two wrong predictions, but their prediction about the Mets was correct. Therefore the Mets could not have finished in sixth place.

6. If the Expos finished sixth, the Phillies were in third and the Cardinals in first.

   A. The Mets made two wrong predictions, and therefore must have finished in second or fourth.

   B. The Pirates were wrong about the Mets. If they were right about the Cubs, they would have had to have finished in fifth; but the Pirates predicted the Cubs would finish fifth. Therefore the Pirates must have been wrong about both the Mets and the Cubs and themselves finished in second or fourth.

   C. By elimination, the Cubs finished fifth.

   D. Step 6C makes the Pirates right about the Cubs, however, which is not possible. Therefore the Expos could not have finished in sixth place.

7. By elimination, the Phillies must have finished in sixth and correctly predicted that the Expos would finish second and the Pirates third.

   A. The Cardinals were right about the Phillies, so they must have finished in fifth.

   B. The Cardinals were wrong about the Cubs finishing fourth, so the Cubs must have finished first.

   C. By elimination, the Mets finished fourth.

Answer:

Standing	Team	Standing	Team
First	Cubs	Fourth	Mets
Second	Expos	Fifth	Cardinals
Third	Pirates	Sixth	Phillies

Solutions to Five Poker Problems

Other answers may be possible. If you have two full house hands, for instance, one with three kings and two queens and the other with three sevens and two sixes, it would be equally valid to put the kings with the sixes, and the queens with the sevens. Abbreviations: d = diamonds, c = clubs, h = hearts, and s = spades.

FIRST POKER PROBLEM

Hand	Cards
First	6d, 5h, 4c, 3c, 2s
Second	Jd, 9d, 7d, 3d, 2d
Third	9s, 8s, 7s, 6s, 3s
Fourth	Kh, Ks, Ah, Ac, As
Fifth	Qh, Qs, 10h, 10s, 10c

SECOND POKER PROBLEM

Hand	Cards
First	Qh, 9h, 7h, 6h, 5h
Second	Kh, Kc, Ks, 4c, 4d
Third	Qs, 9s, 7s, 6s, 3s
Fourth	6d, 5d, 4d, 3d, 2d
Fifth	3c, 3h, 2c, 2h, 2s

THIRD POKER PROBLEM

Hand	Cards
First	7h, 6h, 4h, 3h, 2h
Second	Js, Ks, 8s, 4s, As
Third	4c, 5s, 6c, 7s, 8h
Fourth	Ad, Kd, 9d, 7d, 6d
Fifth	Jh, 10h, 9s, 8c, 7c

FOURTH POKER PROBLEM

Hand	Cards
First	Ac, Qc, 9c, 5c, 2c
Second	Qs, 10s, 6s, 3s, 2s
Third	Ah, 2d, 3c, 4d, 5h
Fourth	Qd, Jd, 10d, 8d, 5d
Fifth	Kh, Qh, Jc, 10c, 9h

FIFTH POKER PROBLEM

Hand	Cards
First	Ad, Kd, Qd, 10d, 8d
Second	Jh, Js, Jc, 2c, 2h
Third	9h, 8h, 7h, 6h, 4h
Fourth	4s, 4d, 5s, 5d, 5c
Fifth	9c, 7c, 6c, Kc, Qc

Solutions to Four Secret Codes (Cryptograms)

FIRST CRYPTOGRAM

The time you invest in your own abilities will return a fine dividend.

SECOND CRYPTOGRAM

One of the hardest things to learn is respect for those who disagree with you.

THIRD CRYPTOGRAM

Somewhere over the rainbow ... an aerosol spray is destroying the ozone layer.

FOURTH CRYPTOGRAM

Modern credit cards: never have so many owed so much to so few.

Solutions to Three History Tests

THE FAMOUS FLASH FLOOD

1. In order for no two persons to have the same number of true statements, and for no one to have made three true statements, the number of true statements per person must have been four, two, one, and none, for a total of seven true statements.
2. If Shem made four true statements (nos. 9–12), then no. 8 is true because no. 10 is, and no. 15 is true because no. 11 is. This makes six true statements. But nos. 3 and 5 and 7 and 14 contradict, yielding two more true statements, for a total of eight. Thus it is impossible for Shem to have made four true statements, since only seven out of the sixteen could be true.
3. If Ham made four true statements (nos. 13–16), then no. 11 is true because no. 15 is, and no. 2 is true because no. 13 is. This makes six true statements. But nos. 3 and 5 and 6 and 9 contradict, yielding two more true statements, for a total of eight. Therefore Ham could not have made four true statements.
4. If Noah made four true statements (nos. 1–4), then no. 13 is true because no. 2 is, making five true statements. Nos. 6 and 9, 7 and 14, and 12 and 16 contradict, making three more true statements, for a total of eight, which is impossible. Therefore Noah could not have made four true statements.
5. By elimination, Mrs. Noah must have made four true statements (nos. 5–8). If no. 8 is true, then no. 10 is true, making five true statements. No. 4 contradicts both nos. 11 and 15, and no. 12 contradicts no. 16. To avoid having more than seven true statements, nos. 2 and 13 must

both be false. Similarly, to avoid having more than seven true statements, no. 4 must be true and both nos. 11 and 15 false. Finally, no. 12 must be true and no. 16 false, since otherwise both Shem and Ham would have one true and three false statements.

Answer:

Statement	True or False	Statement	True or False
1	F	9	F
2	F	10	T
3	F	11	F
4	T	12	T
5	T	13	F
6	T	14	F
7	T	15	F
8	T	16	F

Mrs. Noah did remember to turn off the major faucets.

THE NOTORIOUS NYMPH OF THE NILE

1. No two persons told the same number of lies, therefore someone told three, someone told two, someone one, and someone none.
2. Someone told more lies than Julius, so he did not tell three.
3. Suppose Antony made three false statements:
   A. We know immediately that no. 8 is false and no. 12 true.
   B. Either Cleopatra or her dad made three true statements. Therefore Cleopatra lost her asp in Memphis, making nos. 1 and 11 true and no. 9 false.
   C. Caesar's statement 7 must be true (or he would have three false statements). Cleopatra's statements 2 and 3, then, are false, and her father's statement 10 is true.
   D. This analysis yields two persons, Cleopatra and Julius, with one true statement each, therefore Antony cannot be the one who tells three lies.
4. Suppose Cleopatra's father told three lies:
   A. Since no. 10 is false, nos. 2 and 3 are true and nos. 4 and 7 are false.
   B. Since no. 11 is false, no. 1 is false and no. 9 is true.
   C. This analysis establishes a lie for Cleopatra (no. 1), for Antony (no. 4), and for Julius (no. 7). Therefore nobody can have three true statements and Cleopatra's father cannot be the one who tells three lies.
5. By elimination, Cleopatra must have made three false statements.
   A. We know Cleopatra loves Julius, therefore no. 4 is false and nos. 7 and 10 true.

   B. If no. 1 is false, no. 9 is true and no. 11 is false.
   C. Julius must be the one with three true statements, so nos. 8 and 6 are both true.
   D. Nos. 5 and 12 contradict: one is true, one false. But regardless of which statement is true, we still have one person with two true statements and one with one true statement. Thus all the conditions of the problem are met.

Answer:
Cleopatra loves Julius.

THE GARDEN OF EDEN

1. No two persons had the same number of lies, therefore the number of lies per person (in some order) must be four, three, two, one, and none. Each person makes an accusation, hence the person with four true statements identifies the one who ate the apple.
2. Abel cannot have four true statements since his statements nos. 13 and 16 contradict.
3. Cain cannot have four true statements because his statement no. 12 says the snake never lies, and that would require that two residents of the Garden have four true statements.
4. Therefore either Adam, Eve, or the snake made four true statements. We can construct a table showing all the possibilities:

Who Spoke the Truth (hypothetical)

Statement	Adam	Eve	Snake	Statement	Adam	Eve	Snake
1	T	F	F	11	. . .	F	F
2	T	F	F	12	F	F	T
3	T	F	. . .	13	F	F	F
4	T	F	. . .	14	. . .	T	T
5	F	T	F	15	F	T	. . .
6	T	T	T	16	F	F	F
7	F	T	. . .	17	F	T	T
8	T	T	F	18	F	F	T
9	F	F	F	19	. . .	T	T
10	T	T	T	20	. . .	T	T

5. If all of Adam's statements are true, we can identify the truth or falsehood of sixteen statements, as indicated in the table. Everyone but Adam has at least two lies, leaving nobody with three true statements. The conditions of the problem cannot be met, therefore Adam cannot have four true statements.
6. If all of the snake's statements are true, we can verify fifteen statements.

Again, nobody could have three true statements, so the snake cannot have four true statements.
7. By elimination, Eve must have made four true statements. The snake, then, must have three true statements, therefore no. 14 must be true and nos. 2 and 11 must be false. Adam must have made four false statements, thus no. 15 is true.

Answer:
Adam ate the apple.

Solutions to Two Tournaments

THE ORATORY CONTEST

1. From the specific statements about how someone voted, we can begin to fill in a table:

	Judge					
Contestant	Fred	George	Hal	Ian	Jim	Total
Alice		3				
Beth				5		15
Cindy						
Diane	4	2		1		
Ella					1	

2. The judge who ranked the contestants in alphabetical order must have been Hal, since the distribution of scores in the table precludes George, Ian, and Jim from an alphabetical ranking, and statement 3 says Fred ranked Ella above Diane.
3. The total number of points is 75 (five judges each voting 15 points— 5, 4, 3, 2, and 1). There are five contestants, therefore the mean score per contestant is 15. Thus, in order for each contestant's rank total to be different, the totals must be 13, 14, 15, 16, and 17, or another combination giving an even wider spread between first and last.

   Taking statement 8 into account, we can deduce that George's rankings of Ella and Cindy must have been more than one place apart. Therefore, since we already know his votes on Alice and Diane, George must have ranked Cindy first and Ella either fourth or fifth.
4. Beth has a 2 and a 5. She must have a 1.
   A. The first place must be voted by Fred—Fred's is the only one that is not accounted for.
   B. To have a total of 15, Beth must have a 4 and a 3 from the other two judges (we are given that she does not have two 5's).

C. Since Jim ranked her higher than George, Jim gave her a 3 and George a 4.
5. It follows that George must have placed Ella fifth.
   Now we can fill in more of the table:

| | Judge | | | | | |
Contestant	Fred	George	Hal	Ian	Jim	Total
Alice		3	1			
Beth	1	4	2	5	3	15
Cindy		1	3			
Diane	4	2	4	1		
Ella		5	5		1	

6. Diane must have received her fifth place from Jim.
7. From statement 12 we can conclude that Jim must have given Cindy a 2 and Alice a 4.
8. Fred must have given his 5 to Cindy, since we know she got one, and the other judges' 5's have already been allocated.
9. From statement 3 we can conclude that Fred must have given Alice a 2 and Ella a 3.
   Revising our table once more:

| | Judge | | | | | |
Contestant	Fred	George	Hal	Ian	Jim	Total
Alice	2	3	1		4	
Beth	1	4	2	5	3	15
Cindy	5	1	3		2	
Diane	4	2	4	1	5	16
Ella	3	5	5		1	

10. Only Ian's rankings remain to be determined.
    A. If Ian gives Ella a 2, she would be tied with Diane, so he could not have done that.
    B. If Ian gives Alice a 2, her total is 12, and Ella's is at least 17. But this would not meet the condition of statement 8: switching George's rankings of Cindy and Ella would not put Ella first.
    C. Ian must have put Cindy second. In order to meet the condition of statement 8, Ian must have put Ella third. Therefore Alice got a 4 and her total is 14, Cindy's total is 13, and Ella's is 17. Switching George's rankings of Cindy and Ella would give Ella 13 (and first place) and Cindy 17 (last place).

Answer:
Cindy won first place.

THE DEBATE TOURNAMENT

1. One team is undefeated after round 4, so two teams must have had 3–0 records and met in round 4 (the match was perfect). Similarly, four teams must have had 2–0 records and met in round 3.
2. Since wins equal losses at any point in a tournament, in round 3 there must have been four teams with 2–0 records, four teams with 0–2 records, and four teams with 1–1 records. At this stage in the tournament, an even number of wins is necessary for a perfect matching.
3. Files knows that team 6 has a win and that team 11 has a loss (round 2). These two teams meet in round 3, so team 6 must have lost round 2 and team 11 must have won round 1.
4. Step 3 shows that there is a winner in round 3 for each of three debates: team 6 versus team 11, 1 versus 10, and 4 versus 7. Of the six debates of round 3, two debates must pit teams with 0–2 records against each other. Files gives team 9 a loss in round 3, but team 9 meets team 6 in round 4; so we know team 9 must have had a win in the first two rounds. The debates between teams with 0–2 records must have been team 5 versus team 12 and 8 versus 3.
5. When we account for the losses for teams 3, 5, 8, and 12 in the first two rounds, we learn that teams 4 and 7 were undefeated when they met in round 3, teams 4 and 7 met teams 1 and 10 in round 4, and, since one of the teams meeting in round 4 is undefeated, it follows that teams 1 and 10 were the other two teams with 2–0 records that met in round 3.
6. Teams 2 and 9, then, both had 1–1 records when Files judged them in round 3. He voted for team 2, making its record 2–1 and team 9's 1–2.
7. Teams 2 and 11 met in the fourth round, which means that team 11 had beaten team 6. Entering round 4, team 11's record is 2–1 and team 6's is 1–2.
8. The four teams without victories met in round 3; the same teams met also in round 4. One of the four teams had to pick up two victories in rounds 3 and 4. Team 12 is matched against team 2 in round 5. We know team 2 has two wins because Files voted for it in round 3, its second win. Team 12 therefore won rounds 3 and 4, and team 2 must have lost round 4. (If all but two matches are perfect in round 5, the two imperfect matches must involve the undefeated team and the team with no wins.)
9. We can deduce from step 8 that team 11 won round 4 and had a 3–1 record going into round 5.
10. Similarly, four teams with 2–0 records met in round 3, and the same four teams met in round 4. One of the four teams must have had a 2–2 record going into round 5. Team 1, matched against team 9 in round 5, must have lost two debates, since we know that team 9 has two losses. Team 9 also must have won round 4. If team 1 lost, team 10 must have won round 3, and team 7 won round 4.
11. If team 10 beat team 1 in round 3 and met team 4 in round 4, then team 4 must have won its third round, too.

12. Teams 10 and 4 were the undefeated teams in round 4; going into round 5, one had a 4–0 record and the other a 3–1 record. Therefore their opponents (teams 7 and 11) both had to have 3–1 records.
13. Files judged the debate between teams 11 and 4 in round 5 and declared team 11 the winner. Team 11's final record is 4–1. If team 4 was undefeated going into round 5, its final record is 4–1; if it had a 3–1 record going into round 5, its final record is 3–2. Either way, team 11 is ahead of team 4, with an equal or better won-lost record and higher speaker points.
14. The other contenders for first place are teams 7 and 10, since team 7 had a 3–1 record and team 10 was either 3–1 or 4–0. If team 10 had a 4–0 record, we know it lost round 5, because no undefeated team remained at the end of the tournament. Team 10 is at best 4–1 and therefore behind team 11, since team 11's speaker points are higher.
15. Finally, if team 7 was successful in round 5, defeating team 10 would give it a 4–1 record, but the ranking of team 7's speakers was lower than the ranking of the speakers of team 11.

Answer:
Team 11 should receive the first-place trophy.

Solution to A Final Matrimonial Mess

CONFUSION CONDOMINIUM

1. Begin by constructing a table indicating who is not married to whom.

	Bobby	Ellie	Freddie	Jerry	Kim	Lou	Pat	Ronnie	Terry	Willie
Bobby	X					X	X	X	X	
Ellie		X	X	X	X				X	
Freddie		X	X	X		X	X	X		X
Jerry		X	X	X	X	X		X		X
Kim		X		X	X			X	X	X
Lou	X			X		X	X		X	
Pat	X		X			X	X	X		X
Ronnie	X		X	X	X			X		
Terry	X	X	X		X	X			X	
Willie		X	X	X		X				X

Obviously no one is married to him or herself. Furthermore, we are told that no one mentions his or her spouse in any of the statements.

Note that each piece of information must be entered on the table twice—in both the row and column headed by a person's name—except for where the table indicates that a person would be married to him or herself.

2. From the table we can see that Freddie is not married to Ronnie. Therefore Pat lies with statement 9. Pat's statement 10 must also be a lie, then; hence Willie is the doctor—and a liar. Willie's statement 16 is a lie: Freddie does not tell the truth.

3. Since Freddie lies, Ellie is not married to Ronnie.

4. Lou must have told the truth about Pat not being the poor man; for if Pat were the poor man, then Pat would tell the truth, which contradicts step 2. Therefore Lou's statement 8 is also true, and Bobby is married to Jerry. (It may be helpful at this point to start filling in the table further, using X's for unmarried pairs and O's for married couples.)

5. Since Bobby is married to Jerry, Kim's statement 6 is true—Jerry is not married to Terry.

6. Taking step 4 into account, we know that Ronnie lies in saying that Bobby is married to Kim. Now we have demonstrated that Ronnie, Pat, Willie, and Freddie all lie, so none of them can be married to each other.

7. Consulting our table, we see that Freddie must be married either to Kim or Lou. If Kim is Freddie's spouse:
   A. Then statement 13 is a lie, hence Terry is the fifth liar, and all the others must tell the truth.
   B. Ellie must tell the truth: Kim is married to the rich man, Freddie.
   C. Bobby must tell the truth: Pat is married to Terry.
   D. But from step 7A we know that Terry lies, and since we know Pat lies, Terry and Pat cannot be married to each other.

8. By elimination, Kim is married to Pat.

9. By elimination, Ellie is married to Willie.

10. By elimination, Ronnie is married to Terry.

11. Ellie tells the truth, so Pat is the rich man.

12. Jerry tells the truth, so Freddie is the beggar man.

13. Ronnie lies, so Jerry must be a man, but not the rich man. Since Jerry tells the truth, he must be the poor man.

14. Ronnie is the fifth man—the thief.

Answer:
Ronnie is the thief.

A CATALOG OF SELECTED DOVER BOOKS IN ALL FIELDS OF INTEREST

DRAWINGS OF REMBRANDT, edited by Seymour Slive. Updated Lippmann, Hofstede de Groot edition, with definitive scholarly apparatus. All portraits, biblical sketches, landscapes, nudes. Oriental figures, classical studies, together with selection of work by followers. 550 illustrations. Total of 630pp. 9⅛ × 12¼.
21485-0, 21486-9 Pa., Two-vol. set $25.00

GHOST AND HORROR STORIES OF AMBROSE BIERCE, Ambrose Bierce. 24 tales vividly imagined, strangely prophetic, and decades ahead of their time in technical skill: "The Damned Thing," "An Inhabitant of Carcosa," "The Eyes of the Panther," "Moxon's Master," and 20 more. 199pp. 5⅜ × 8½. 20767-6 Pa. $3.95

ETHICAL WRITINGS OF MAIMONIDES, Maimonides. Most significant ethical works of great medieval sage, newly translated for utmost precision, readability. Laws Concerning Character Traits, Eight Chapters, more. 192pp. 5⅜ × 8½.
24522-5 Pa. $4.50

THE EXPLORATION OF THE COLORADO RIVER AND ITS CANYONS, J. W. Powell. Full text of Powell's 1,000-mile expedition down the fabled Colorado in 1869. Superb account of terrain, geology, vegetation, Indians, famine, mutiny, treacherous rapids, mighty canyons, during exploration of last unknown part of continental U.S. 400pp. 5⅜ × 8½. 20094-9 Pa. $6.95

HISTORY OF PHILOSOPHY, Julián Marías. Clearest one-volume history on the market. Every major philosopher and dozens of others, to Existentialism and later. 505pp. 5⅜ × 8½. 21739-6 Pa. $8.50

ALL ABOUT LIGHTNING, Martin A. Uman. Highly readable non-technical survey of nature and causes of lightning, thunderstorms, ball lightning, St. Elmo's Fire, much more. Illustrated. 192pp. 5⅜ × 8½. 25237-X Pa. $5.95

SAILING ALONE AROUND THE WORLD, Captain Joshua Slocum. First man to sail around the world, alone, in small boat. One of great feats of seamanship told in delightful manner. 67 illustrations. 294pp. 5⅜ × 8½. 20326-3 Pa. $4.95

LETTERS AND NOTES ON THE MANNERS, CUSTOMS AND CONDITIONS OF THE NORTH AMERICAN INDIANS, George Catlin. Classic account of life among Plains Indians: ceremonies, hunt, warfare, etc. 312 plates. 572pp. of text. 6⅛ × 9¼. 22118-0, 22119-9 Pa. Two-vol. set $15.90

ALASKA: The Harriman Expedition, 1899, John Burroughs, John Muir, et al. Informative, engrossing accounts of two-month, 9,000-mile expedition. Native peoples, wildlife, forests, geography, salmon industry, glaciers, more. Profusely illustrated. 240 black-and-white line drawings. 124 black-and-white photographs. 3 maps. Index. 576pp. 5⅜ × 8½. 25109-8 Pa. $11.95

ILLUSTRATED DICTIONARY OF HISTORIC ARCHITECTURE, edited by Cyril M. Harris. Extraordinary compendium of clear, concise definitions for over 5,000 important architectural terms complemented by over 2,000 line drawings. Covers full spectrum of architecture from ancient ruins to 20th-century Modernism. Preface. 592pp. 7½ × 9⅝. 24444-X Pa. $14.95

THE NIGHT BEFORE CHRISTMAS, Clement Moore. Full text, and woodcuts from original 1848 book. Also critical, historical material. 19 illustrations. 40pp. 4⅝ × 6. 22797-9 Pa. $2.50

THE LESSON OF JAPANESE ARCHITECTURE: 165 Photographs, Jiro Harada. Memorable gallery of 165 photographs taken in the 1930's of exquisite Japanese homes of the well-to-do and historic buildings. 13 line diagrams. 192pp. 8⅝ × 11¼. 24778-3 Pa. $8.95

THE AUTOBIOGRAPHY OF CHARLES DARWIN AND SELECTED LETTERS, edited by Francis Darwin. The fascinating life of eccentric genius composed of an intimate memoir by Darwin (intended for his children); commentary by his son, Francis; hundreds of fragments from notebooks, journals, papers; and letters to and from Lyell, Hooker, Huxley, Wallace and Henslow. xi + 365pp. 5⅜ × 8. 20479-0 Pa. $5.95

WONDERS OF THE SKY: Observing Rainbows, Comets, Eclipses, the Stars and Other Phenomena, Fred Schaaf. Charming, easy-to-read poetic guide to all manner of celestial events visible to the naked eye. Mock suns, glories, Belt of Venus, more. Illustrated. 299pp. 5¼ × 8¼. 24402-4 Pa. $7.95

BURNHAM'S CELESTIAL HANDBOOK, Robert Burnham, Jr. Thorough guide to the stars beyond our solar system. Exhaustive treatment. Alphabetical by constellation: Andromeda to Cetus in Vol. 1; Chamaeleon to Orion in Vol. 2; and Pavo to Vulpecula in Vol. 3. Hundreds of illustrations. Index in Vol. 3. 2,000pp. 6⅛ × 9¼. 23567-X, 23568-8, 23673-0 Pa., Three-vol. set $37.85

STAR NAMES: Their Lore and Meaning, Richard Hinckley Allen. Fascinating history of names various cultures have given to constellations and literary and folkloristic uses that have been made of stars. Indexes to subjects. Arabic and Greek names. Biblical references. Bibliography. 563pp. 5⅜ × 8½. 21079-0 Pa. $7.95

THIRTY YEARS THAT SHOOK PHYSICS: The Story of Quantum Theory, George Gamow. Lucid, accessible introduction to influential theory of energy and matter. Careful explanations of Dirac's anti-particles, Bohr's model of the atom, much more. 12 plates. Numerous drawings. 240pp. 5⅜ × 8½. 24895-X Pa. $4.95

CHINESE DOMESTIC FURNITURE IN PHOTOGRAPHS AND MEASURED DRAWINGS, Gustav Ecke. A rare volume, now affordably priced for antique collectors, furniture buffs and art historians. Detailed review of styles ranging from early Shang to late Ming. Unabridged republication. 161 black-and-white drawings, photos. Total of 224pp. 8⅜ × 11¼. (Available in U.S. only) 25171-3 Pa. $12.95

VINCENT VAN GOGH: A Biography, Julius Meier-Graefe. Dynamic, penetrating study of artist's life, relationship with brother, Theo, painting techniques, travels, more. Readable, engrossing. 160pp. 5⅜ × 8½. (Available in U.S. only) 25253-1 Pa. $3.95

HOW TO WRITE, Gertrude Stein. Gertrude Stein claimed anyone could understand her unconventional writing—here are clues to help. Fascinating improvisations, language experiments, explanations illuminate Stein's craft and the art of writing. Total of 414pp. 4⅜ × 6⅜. 23144-5 Pa. $5.95

ADVENTURES AT SEA IN THE GREAT AGE OF SAIL: Five Firsthand Narratives, edited by Elliot Snow. Rare true accounts of exploration, whaling, shipwreck, fierce natives, trade, shipboard life, more. 33 illustrations. Introduction. 353pp. 5⅜ × 8½. 25177-2 Pa. $7.95

THE HERBAL OR GENERAL HISTORY OF PLANTS, John Gerard. Classic descriptions of about 2,850 plants—with over 2,700 illustrations—includes Latin and English names, physical descriptions, varieties, time and place of growth, more. 2,706 illustrations. xlv + 1,678pp. 8½ × 12¼. 23147-X Cloth. $75.00

DOROTHY AND THE WIZARD IN OZ, L. Frank Baum. Dorothy and the Wizard visit the center of the Earth, where people are vegetables, glass houses grow and Oz characters reappear. Classic sequel to *Wizard of Oz*. 256pp. 5⅜ × 8. 24714-7 Pa. $4.95

SONGS OF EXPERIENCE: Facsimile Reproduction with 26 Plates in Full Color, William Blake. This facsimile of Blake's original "Illuminated Book" reproduces 26 full-color plates from a rare 1826 edition. Includes "The Tyger," "London," "Holy Thursday," and other immortal poems. 26 color plates. Printed text of poems. 48pp. 5¼ × 7. 24636-1 Pa. $3.50

SONGS OF INNOCENCE, William Blake. The first and most popular of Blake's famous "Illuminated Books," in a facsimile edition reproducing all 31 brightly colored plates. Additional printed text of each poem. 64pp. 5¼ × 7. 22764-2 Pa. $3.50

PRECIOUS STONES, Max Bauer. Classic, thorough study of diamonds, rubies, emeralds, garnets, etc.: physical character, occurrence, properties, use, similar topics. 20 plates, 8 in color. 94 figures. 659pp. 6⅛ × 9¼. 21910-0, 21911-9 Pa., Two-vol. set $15.90

ENCYCLOPEDIA OF VICTORIAN NEEDLEWORK, S. F. A. Caulfeild and Blanche Saward. Full, precise descriptions of stitches, techniques for dozens of needlecrafts—most exhaustive reference of its kind. Over 800 figures. Total of 679pp. 8⅛ × 11. Two volumes. Vol. 1 22800-2 Pa. $11.95
Vol. 2 22801-0 Pa. $11.95

THE MARVELOUS LAND OF OZ, L. Frank Baum. Second Oz book, the Scarecrow and Tin Woodman are back with hero named Tip, Oz magic. 136 illustrations. 287pp. 5⅜ × 8½. 20692-0 Pa. $5.95

WILD FOWL DECOYS, Joel Barber. Basic book on the subject, by foremost authority and collector. Reveals history of decoy making and rigging, place in American culture, different kinds of decoys, how to make them, and how to use them. 140 plates. 156pp. 7⅞ × 10¾. 20011-6 Pa. $8.95

HISTORY OF LACE, Mrs. Bury Palliser. Definitive, profusely illustrated chronicle of lace from earliest times to late 19th century. Laces of Italy, Greece, England, France, Belgium, etc. Landmark of needlework scholarship. 266 illustrations. 672pp. 6⅛ × 9¼. 24742-2 Pa. $14.95

SUNDIALS, Albert Waugh. Far and away the best, most thorough coverage of ideas, mathematics concerned, types, construction, adjusting anywhere. Over 100 illustrations. 230pp. 5⅜ × 8½. 22947-5 Pa. $4.50

PICTURE HISTORY OF THE NORMANDIE: With 190 Illustrations, Frank O. Braynard. Full story of legendary French ocean liner: Art Deco interiors, design innovations, furnishings, celebrities, maiden voyage, tragic fire, much more. Extensive text. 144pp. 8⅞ × 11¾. 25257-4 Pa. $9.95

THE FIRST AMERICAN COOKBOOK: A Facsimile of "American Cookery," 1796, Amelia Simmons. Facsimile of the first American-written cookbook published in the United States contains authentic recipes for colonial favorites—pumpkin pudding, winter squash pudding, spruce beer, Indian slapjacks, and more. Introductory Essay and Glossary of colonial cooking terms. 80pp. 5⅜ × 8½. 24710-4 Pa. $3.50

101 PUZZLES IN THOUGHT AND LOGIC, C. R. Wylie, Jr. Solve murders and robberies, find out which fishermen are liars, how a blind man could possibly identify a color—purely by your own reasoning! 107pp. 5⅜ × 8½. 20367-0 Pa. $2.50

THE BOOK OF WORLD-FAMOUS MUSIC—CLASSICAL, POPULAR AND FOLK, James J. Fuld. Revised and enlarged republication of landmark work in musico-bibliography. Full information about nearly 1,000 songs and compositions including first lines of music and lyrics. New supplement. Index. 800pp. 5⅜ × 8¼. 24857-7 Pa. $14.95

ANTHROPOLOGY AND MODERN LIFE, Franz Boas. Great anthropologist's classic treatise on race and culture. Introduction by Ruth Bunzel. Only inexpensive paperback edition. 255pp. 5⅜ × 8½. 25245-0 Pa. $5.95

THE TALE OF PETER RABBIT, Beatrix Potter. The inimitable Peter's terrifying adventure in Mr. McGregor's garden, with all 27 wonderful, full-color Potter illustrations. 55pp. 4¼ × 5½. (Available in U.S. only) 22827-4 Pa. $1.75

THREE PROPHETIC SCIENCE FICTION NOVELS, H. G. Wells. *When the Sleeper Wakes, A Story of the Days to Come* and *The Time Machine* (full version). 335pp. 5⅜ × 8½. (Available in U.S. only) 20605-X Pa. $5.95

APICIUS COOKERY AND DINING IN IMPERIAL ROME, edited and translated by Joseph Dommers Vehling. Oldest known cookbook in existence offers readers a clear picture of what foods Romans ate, how they prepared them, etc. 49 illustrations. 301pp. 6⅛ × 9¼. 23563-7 Pa. $6.50

SHAKESPEARE LEXICON AND QUOTATION DICTIONARY, Alexander Schmidt. Full definitions, locations, shades of meaning of every word in plays and poems. More than 50,000 exact quotations. 1,485pp. 6½ × 9¼. 22726-X, 22727-8 Pa., Two-vol. set $27.90

THE WORLD'S GREAT SPEECHES, edited by Lewis Copeland and Lawrence W. Lamm. Vast collection of 278 speeches from Greeks to 1970. Powerful and effective models; unique look at history. 842pp. 5⅜ × 8½. 20468-5 Pa. $11.95

CHRISTMAS CUSTOMS AND TRADITIONS, Clement A. Miles. Origin, evolution, significance of religious, secular practices. Caroling, gifts, yule logs, much more. Full, scholarly yet fascinating; non-sectarian. 400pp. 5⅜ × 8½.
23354-5 Pa. $6.50

THE HUMAN FIGURE IN MOTION, Eadweard Muybridge. More than 4,500 stopped-action photos, in action series, showing undraped men, women, children jumping, lying down, throwing, sitting, wrestling, carrying, etc. 390pp. 7⅞ × 10⅝.
20204-6 Cloth. $19.95

THE MAN WHO WAS THURSDAY, Gilbert Keith Chesterton. Witty, fast-paced novel about a club of anarchists in turn-of-the-century London. Brilliant social, religious, philosophical speculations. 128pp. 5⅜ × 8½.
25121-7 Pa. $3.95

A CEZANNE SKETCHBOOK: Figures, Portraits, Landscapes and Still Lifes, Paul Cezanne. Great artist experiments with tonal effects, light, mass, other qualities in over 100 drawings. A revealing view of developing master painter, precursor of Cubism. 102 black-and-white illustrations. 144pp. 8¾ × 6⅝.
24790-2 Pa. $5.95

AN ENCYCLOPEDIA OF BATTLES: Accounts of Over 1,560 Battles from 1479 B.C. to the Present, David Eggenberger. Presents essential details of every major battle in recorded history, from the first battle of Megiddo in 1479 B.C. to Grenada in 1984. List of Battle Maps. New Appendix covering the years 1967–1984. Index. 99 illustrations. 544pp. 6½ × 9¼.
24913-1 Pa. $14.95

AN ETYMOLOGICAL DICTIONARY OF MODERN ENGLISH, Ernest Weekley. Richest, fullest work, by foremost British lexicographer. Detailed word histories. Inexhaustible. Total of 856pp. 6½ × 9¼.
21873-2, 21874-0 Pa., Two-vol. set $17.00

WEBSTER'S AMERICAN MILITARY BIOGRAPHIES, edited by Robert McHenry. Over 1,000 figures who shaped 3 centuries of American military history. Detailed biographies of Nathan Hale, Douglas MacArthur, Mary Hallaren, others. Chronologies of engagements, more. Introduction. Addenda. 1,033 entries in alphabetical order. xi + 548pp. 6½ × 9¼. (Available in U.S. only)
24758-9 Pa. $11.95

LIFE IN ANCIENT EGYPT, Adolf Erman. Detailed older account, with much not in more recent books: domestic life, religion, magic, medicine, commerce, and whatever else needed for complete picture. Many illustrations. 597pp. 5⅜ × 8½.
22632-8 Pa. $8.95

HISTORIC COSTUME IN PICTURES, Braun & Schneider. Over 1,450 costumed figures shown, covering a wide variety of peoples: kings, emperors, nobles, priests, servants, soldiers, scholars, townsfolk, peasants, merchants, courtiers, cavaliers, and more. 256pp. 8⅜ × 11¼.
23150-X Pa. $7.95

THE NOTEBOOKS OF LEONARDO DA VINCI, edited by J. P. Richter. Extracts from manuscripts reveal great genius; on painting, sculpture, anatomy, sciences, geography, etc. Both Italian and English. 186 ms. pages reproduced, plus 500 additional drawings, including studies for *Last Supper*, *Sforza* monument, etc. 860pp. 7⅞ × 10¾. (Available in U.S. only) 22572-0, 22573-9 Pa., Two-vol. set $25.90

THE ART NOUVEAU STYLE BOOK OF ALPHONSE MUCHA: All 72 Plates from "Documents Decoratifs" in Original Color, Alphonse Mucha. Rare copyright-free design portfolio by high priest of Art Nouveau. Jewelry, wallpaper, stained glass, furniture, figure studies, plant and animal motifs, etc. Only complete one-volume edition. 80pp. 9⅜ × 12¼. 24044-4 Pa. $8.95

ANIMALS: 1,419 COPYRIGHT-FREE ILLUSTRATIONS OF MAMMALS, BIRDS, FISH, INSECTS, ETC., edited by Jim Harter. Clear wood engravings present, in extremely lifelike poses, over 1,000 species of animals. One of the most extensive pictorial sourcebooks of its kind. Captions. Index. 284pp. 9 × 12. 23766-4 Pa. $9.95

OBELISTS FLY HIGH, C. Daly King. Masterpiece of American detective fiction, long out of print, involves murder on a 1935 transcontinental flight—"a very thrilling story"—NY Times. Unabridged and unaltered republication of the edition published by William Collins Sons & Co. Ltd., London, 1935. 288pp. 5⅜ × 8½. (Available in U.S. only) 25036-9 Pa. $4.95

VICTORIAN AND EDWARDIAN FASHION: A Photographic Survey, Alison Gernsheim. First fashion history completely illustrated by contemporary photographs. Full text plus 235 photos, 1840–1914, in which many celebrities appear. 240pp. 6½ × 9¼. 24205-6 Pa. $6.00

THE ART OF THE FRENCH ILLUSTRATED BOOK, 1700–1914, Gordon N. Ray. Over 630 superb book illustrations by Fragonard, Delacroix, Daumier, Doré, Grandville, Manet, Mucha, Steinlen, Toulouse-Lautrec and many others. Preface. Introduction. 633 halftones. Indices of artists, authors & titles, binders and provenances. Appendices. Bibliography. 608pp. 8⅜ × 11¼. 25086-5 Pa. $24.95

THE WONDERFUL WIZARD OF OZ, L. Frank Baum. Facsimile in full color of America's finest children's classic. 143 illustrations by W. W. Denslow. 267pp. 5⅜ × 8½. 20691-2 Pa. $5.95

FRONTIERS OF MODERN PHYSICS: New Perspectives on Cosmology, Relativity, Black Holes and Extraterrestrial Intelligence, Tony Rothman, et al. For the intelligent layman. Subjects include: cosmological models of the universe; black holes; the neutrino; the search for extraterrestrial intelligence. Introduction. 46 black-and-white illustrations. 192pp. 5⅜ × 8½. 24587-X Pa. $6.95

THE FRIENDLY STARS, Martha Evans Martin & Donald Howard Menzel. Classic text marshalls the stars together in an engaging, non-technical survey, presenting them as sources of beauty in night sky. 23 illustrations. Foreword. 2 star charts. Index. 147pp. 5⅜ × 8½. 21099-5 Pa. $3.50

FADS AND FALLACIES IN THE NAME OF SCIENCE, Martin Gardner. Fair, witty appraisal of cranks, quacks, and quackeries of science and pseudoscience: hollow earth, Velikovsky, orgone energy, Dianetics, flying saucers, Bridey Murphy, food and medical fads, etc. Revised, expanded In the Name of Science. "A very able and even-tempered presentation."—The New Yorker. 363pp. 5⅜ × 8. 20394-8 Pa. $6.50

ANCIENT EGYPT: ITS CULTURE AND HISTORY, J. E Manchip White. From pre-dynastics through Ptolemies: society, history, political structure, religion, daily life, literature, cultural heritage. 48 plates. 217pp. 5⅜ × 8½. 22548-8 Pa. $4.95

SIR HARRY HOTSPUR OF HUMBLETHWAITE, Anthony Trollope. Incisive, unconventional psychological study of a conflict between a wealthy baronet, his idealistic daughter, and their scapegrace cousin. The 1870 novel in its first inexpensive edition in years. 250pp. 5⅜ × 8½. 24953-0 Pa. $5.95

LASERS AND HOLOGRAPHY, Winston E. Kock. Sound introduction to burgeoning field, expanded (1981) for second edition. Wave patterns, coherence, lasers, diffraction, zone plates, properties of holograms, recent advances. 84 illustrations. 160pp. 5⅜ × 8¼. (Except in United Kingdom) 24041-X Pa. $3.50

INTRODUCTION TO ARTIFICIAL INTELLIGENCE: SECOND, EN-LARGED EDITION, Philip C. Jackson, Jr. Comprehensive survey of artificial intelligence—the study of how machines (computers) can be made to act intelligently. Includes introductory and advanced material. Extensive notes updating the main text. 132 black-and-white illustrations. 512pp. 5⅜ × 8½. 24864-X Pa. $8.95

HISTORY OF INDIAN AND INDONESIAN ART, Ananda K. Coomaraswamy. Over 400 illustrations illuminate classic study of Indian art from earliest Harappa finds to early 20th century. Provides philosophical, religious and social insights. 304pp. 6⅝ × 9⅜. 25005-9 Pa. $8.95

THE GOLEM, Gustav Meyrink. Most famous supernatural novel in modern European literature, set in Ghetto of Old Prague around 1890. Compelling story of mystical experiences, strange transformations, profound terror. 13 black-and-white illustrations. 224pp. 5⅜ × 8½. (Available in U.S. only) 25025-3 Pa. $5.95

ARMADALE, Wilkie Collins. Third great mystery novel by the author of The Woman in White and The Moonstone. Original magazine version with 40 illustrations. 597pp. 5⅜ × 8½. 23429-0 Pa. $9.95

PICTORIAL ENCYCLOPEDIA OF HISTORIC ARCHITECTURAL PLANS, DETAILS AND ELEMENTS: With 1,880 Line Drawings of Arches, Domes, Doorways, Facades, Gables, Windows, etc., John Theodore Haneman. Sourcebook of inspiration for architects, designers, others. Bibliography. Captions. 141pp. 9 × 12. 24605-1 Pa. $6.95

BENCHLEY LOST AND FOUND, Robert Benchley. Finest humor from early 30's, about pet peeves, child psychologists, post office and others. Mostly unavailable elsewhere. 73 illustrations by Peter Arno and others. 183pp. 5⅜ × 8½. 22410-4 Pa. $3.95

ERTÉ GRAPHICS, Erté. Collection of striking color graphics: Seasons, Alphabet, Numerals, Aces and Precious Stones. 50 plates, including 4 on covers. 48pp. 9⅜ × 12¼. 23580-7 Pa. $6.95

THE JOURNAL OF HENRY D. THOREAU, edited by Bradford Torrey, F. H. Allen. Complete reprinting of 14 volumes, 1837–61, over two million words; the sourcebooks for Walden, etc. Definitive. All original sketches, plus 75 photographs. 1,804pp. 8½ × 12¼. 20312-3, 20313-1 Cloth., Two-vol. set $80.00

CASTLES: THEIR CONSTRUCTION AND HISTORY, Sidney Toy. Traces castle development from ancient roots. Nearly 200 photographs and drawings illustrate moats, keeps, baileys, many other features. Caernarvon, Dover Castles, Hadrian's Wall, Tower of London, dozens more. 256pp. 5⅜ × 8¼. 24898-4 Pa. $5.95

AMERICAN CLIPPER SHIPS: 1833-1858, Octavius T. Howe & Frederick C. Matthews. Fully-illustrated, encyclopedic review of 352 clipper ships from the period of America's greatest maritime supremacy. Introduction. 109 halftones. 5 black-and-white line illustrations. Index. Total of 928pp. 5⅜ × 8½.
25115-2, 25116-0 Pa., Two-vol. set $17.90

TOWARDS A NEW ARCHITECTURE, Le Corbusier. Pioneering manifesto by great architect, near legendary founder of "International School." Technical and aesthetic theories, views on industry, economics, relation of form to function, "mass-production spirit," much more. Profusely illustrated. Unabridged translation of 13th French edition. Introduction by Frederick Etchells. 320pp. 6⅛ × 9¼. (Available in U.S. only)
25023-7 Pa. $8.95

THE BOOK OF KELLS, edited by Blanche Cirker. Inexpensive collection of 32 full-color, full-page plates from the greatest illuminated manuscript of the Middle Ages, painstakingly reproduced from rare facsimile edition. Publisher's Note. Captions. 32pp. 9⅜ × 12¼.
24345-1 Pa. $4.95

BEST SCIENCE FICTION STORIES OF H. G. WELLS, H. G. Wells. Full novel *The Invisible Man*, plus 17 short stories: "The Crystal Egg," "Aepyornis Island," "The Strange Orchid," etc. 303pp. 5⅜ × 8½. (Available in U.S. only)
21531-8 Pa. $4.95

AMERICAN SAILING SHIPS: Their Plans and History, Charles G. Davis. Photos, construction details of schooners, frigates, clippers, other sailcraft of 18th to early 20th centuries—plus entertaining discourse on design, rigging, nautical lore, much more. 137 black-and-white illustrations. 240pp. 6⅛ × 9¼.
24658-2 Pa. $5.95

ENTERTAINING MATHEMATICAL PUZZLES, Martin Gardner. Selection of author's favorite conundrums involving arithmetic, money, speed, etc., with lively commentary. Complete solutions. 112pp. 5⅜ × 8½. 25211-6 Pa. $2.95

THE WILL TO BELIEVE, HUMAN IMMORTALITY, William James. Two books bound together. Effect of irrational on logical, and arguments for human immortality. 402pp. 5⅜ × 8½. 20291-7 Pa. $7.50

THE HAUNTED MONASTERY and THE CHINESE MAZE MURDERS, Robert Van Gulik. 2 full novels by Van Gulik continue adventures of Judge Dee and his companions. An evil Taoist monastery, seemingly supernatural events; overgrown topiary maze that hides strange crimes. Set in 7th-century China. 27 illustrations. 328pp. 5⅜ × 8½. 23502-5 Pa. $5.95

CELEBRATED CASES OF JUDGE DEE (DEE GOONG AN), translated by Robert Van Gulik. Authentic 18th-century Chinese detective novel; Dee and associates solve three interlocked cases. Led to Van Gulik's own stories with same characters. Extensive introduction. 9 illustrations. 237pp. 5⅜ × 8½.
23337-5 Pa. $4.95

Prices subject to change without notice.
Available at your book dealer or write for free catalog to Dept. GI, Dover Publications, Inc., 31 East 2nd St., Mineola, N.Y. 11501. Dover publishes more than 175 books each year on science, elementary and advanced mathematics, biology, music, art, literary history, social sciences and other areas.